Another Kind of Love

Another Kind of Love

HOMOSEXUALITY AND SPIRITUALITY

Richard Woods, O.P.

THIRD EDITION

KNOLL PUBLISHING CO., INC.
1988

Knoll Publishing Co., Inc.
831 W. Washington Blvd.
Ft. Wayne, IN 46802

Library of Congress Cataloging in Publication Data

Library of Congress Catalog Number 88-80107
ISBN 0-940267-06-3

Contents

Introduction

WHEN this book appeared in 1977, it evoked widespread critical reaction, as the saying goes. Not that there were many notices. Some were very brief. Rather, the *range* of responses was extensive — from warm endorsement to icy horror. It was dismissed as both outrageous and naive, and it was welcomed as a balanced treatment of a highly controversial issue.

Shortly after the book was published, I also began receiving personal letters. The overall message of the ordinary men and women for whom the book had been written was modest and simple. In effect, they said, "Thanks." Somewhat surprisingly, I received only one unfavorable letter.

The invitation a year later to prepare a revised edition for Image Books was therefore doubly welcome. For it gave me the opportunity to profit from the critical reviews and to reach a wider audience. I added some new material — most notably the chapter on spirituality. I also attempted to remedy the weakness of the first edition with regard to gay women, information about whose lives and experience has only slowly gained the recognition and study that has been available for many years with regard to male experience, itself still relatively scant and episodic.

When Joel Wells first invited me to write the book, it was intended for the Thomas More Press "Living with" series. The decision to change the format and the title to *Another Kind of Love* bothered me at first because it seemed to oppose homosexual love to heterosexual love. I felt that what was essential about human love applied equally to both gay and straight persons, and to men and women. Eventually, I became more comfortable with the change. I am still convinced that all human love is fundamentally the same. Gay men and women are above all human. Their lives and loving, faith and hope, are no different from those of anyone else. However, *within* the common human condition, the situation and thus the expression of gay love are often significantly different from those of straight persons. It is important to recognize those differences as well as the common elements of experience — and that is what the title in fact suggests.

Several objections were lodged against the subtitle, mainly to the effect that I nowhere treated spirituality directly. This observation was valid. As an essay *in* spirituality, not *about* it, the book as a whole was intended to reflect, not examine, the spirituality of gay women and men. The chapter originally entitled "Gay Spirituality" was to that extent admittedly misleading, so I added a new chapter on spirituality to the second edition. This third edition has allowed me to integrate that material more carefully.

For reasons that will emerge later, I still believe that a distinctive spirituality, like those of other special groups of Christians set apart by circumstances (e.g., single parents, divorced persons, recovering alcoholics, priests, the military, prisoners, members of 'secular' institutes, etc.) already resides in the fundamental life experience of women and men who happen to be gay. As with all such implicit spiritualities, the constitutive elements must be brought to awareness by a process of interpretation. No one book, no one writer, will be able to achieve that task for the simple reason that all spiritualities are both pluralistic and social. Thus, there are not only many dimensions of gay spirituality, there are many different spiritualities latent in the gay world. The process of explicitating them will be a long, difficult, and, above all, a collective one.

My discussion of language also aroused some dissidence, especially in the gay press. Most of the disagreement revolved around two issues which warrant a further word — the use of the words "gay" and "lesbian," and the matter of cross-gender references as a form of gay slang or "camp." The demand by some lesbians that "gay" be restricted to males, while an understandable position in terms of the need for greater visibility among women in the gay world (and the straight world), is, I am still convinced, self-defeating. For one thing, "gay" customarily referred to both men and women and in fact may have originally referred mainly to women. "Gay" signifies a form of consciousness, a way of approaching things, including life in general. It can thus function as a unifying term, as in "gay liberation," avoiding the sexist implications of a world already too embroiled in gender conflicts. (I must add that since 1978, the political and social rift between gay women and men has widened under both feminist and anti-feminist pressure in the homosexual world as well as the wider community. The AIDS epidemic, on the other hand, has tended to unify homosexual men and women, even though lesbians seem to represent the lowest "at risk" group in the population as a whole.)

The second issue concerns my unfavorable attitude toward "camp." Blacks can call each other "nigger" without inciting a riot. Gay men can call each other "faggot" without offense, even though in both cases mild irony or some kind of affectionate criticism is being conveyed. In Western society, however, to refer derogatorily to a man in feminine terms is a mutually offensive slur, reflecting one of the ugliest facets of our male-dominated, deeply insecure culture. The inability of many gay men to grasp this is itself a symptom of how deeply embedded sexist bias can be in all segments of modern life.

Here I would direct attention to the pointed discussion in *the David Kopay Story*,[1] in which the gay former all-star football player describes not merely how professional athletes humiliate and taunt each other by such references, but also the scorn and fear of women that lurks behind it. The ratification by gay men of such prejudicial use of feminine references in the straight world is not merely a capitulation to the same 'macho' bias that despises "queers." It also manifests an ambivalent or even hostile attitude toward women — gay as well as straight. It is at best profoundly insensitive and may well betray a deep fear of women that *is* spiritually and psychologically pathological.

As Del Martin and Phyllis Lyon point out in *Lesbian/Woman*, a belief in the inferior status of women even in lesbian culture found expression a generation ago in the form of an exaggerated masculine appearance and life-style affected by some women.[2] Even today lesbians are not free from gender-crossing camp, if they are less derogatory about it than gay men.[3] The women's liberation movement has brought about a decline in such symbolic and possibly unconscious self-depreciation. But both lesbians and male gays still have a ways further to go.

Another criticism concerned the short shrift I gave lesbians in general. Admittedly, there was no chapter devoted to lesbian experience — and still isn't. I attempted to note those facts of gay experience that pertained especially to lesbians, but the fact is that women are (still) sadly under-represented in research articles as well as membership in Dignity and similar organizations. The reasons for this, as explained in the book, are manifold.

I lengthened the lesbian shrift in the second edition by enlarging sections that were too brief and adding others where appropriate without, I hope, exceeding the limits of my grasp of the lesbian situation. But as a man and a churchman at that, I have to confess that my grasp *is* deficient and will probably remain so. Consequently, the concerned critic should continue to agitate not only for my on-going education but for a thorough discussion of lesbian spirituality from a feminine viewpoint.[4]

Much more, of course, can and will be said and written about both male and female homosexuality from a spiritual and pastoral perspective. In several respects, my own views have changed from what they were when I began this book in 1976.

Rather than attempt to add it all to *Another Kind of Love,* however, I would draw the reader's attention to the resources listed at the end of this book. There is one exception. In 1978, when the second edition of this book was published, no one had yet heard of Acquired Immune Deficiency Syndrome (AIDS) — now a dreaded worldwide epidemic. Even today, there are only a handful of books on the subject and its relationship to Christian life — among which I must single out Eileen Flynn's *AIDS: A Catholic Call for Compassion,* John Fortunato's *AIDS: The Spiritual Dilemma,* and especially and most recently Vicky Cosstick's *AIDS: Meeting the Community Challenge.*[5] Because of the devastating effect of AIDS on the homosexual population in North America and Europe, as well as the resulting and hostile new perception of homosexuality in the heterosexual world as a health threat, it would have been unthinkable to reprint *Another Kind of Love* without reference to this situation. In some respects, the entire book has been recast in the somber light cast by AIDS and its consequences.

AIDS is not the most important issue in the perplexed area of homosexuality and spirituality, but it is for now a very urgent one. And when (soon, please God) AIDS will be only a painfilled memory, the problems of understanding, acceptance, and integration will remain to perplex both gay and straight Christians in every walk of life.

Other considerations also prompted me to set aside the time to revise the second edition. I received many more letters after its publication — most were positive, written in gratitude by the parents, friends, and even the children of gay men and women as well as gays and lesbians themselves who had been reached by the Image edition. And although that has now been out of print for over three years, I still receive letters from people whose lives were touched in some way by reading a friend's copy, or even a photocopy, and wanted to tell me about it. More often, I receive letters from men and women unable to find a copy.

There were also some unfavorable responses, one of them written on behalf of the Congregation for the Doctrine of the

Faith, which found a few passages objectionable for a variety of reasons. Since these were minor points and did not affect the central message of the book, which was recognized by the censor as "having much of value," I have recast them in the present edition to prevent misunderstandings.

Back in 1976, when Joel Wells first suggested the idea of a book on homosexuality and Christian life to me, he expressed a strong desire to avoid theological controversy in order to deal with the spiritual and pastoral problems encountered by ordinary people — the families, pastors, teachers, and friends of gay and lesbian Christians. I still believe this to be a wise course.

Moral and theological issues are entailed, of course, in all pastoral practice, including this book. After all, ministry is a dialectical process in which the demands of the apostolate often require theoretical reconsideration. These in turn lead to new approaches in ministry. Given the wide range of opinion on most of the issues involved, some controversy will attend almost any statement on the subject. But if anything I have written here might be construed to contravene the Biblical witness to God's revelation or the authentic interpretation of that revelation by the Church, that is both unintentional and undesired.

I dedicated the second edition of this book to two pioneers in Catholic ministry to the gay members of Christ's body — Mary Houlihan, who died in 1977, and John McNeill, then a member of the Society of Jesus, the publication of whose ground-breaking book *The Church and the Homosexual* was still being delayed by censors. Ten years later, I would add to their names such a host of friends and co-workers in ministry that it would require several pages to list them. I have selected, rather, a number of friends from the medical, pastoral, and theological communities who have provided support and encouragement, and whose lives — and in some instances, deaths — symbolize for me the vast cloud of witnesses to the mysterious compassion of God: Douglas Branch, M.D., Domeena Renshaw, M.D., William Nelson, R.N., Drs. Jim and Evelyn Whitehead, Dan

Berrigan, S.J., Dr. Jim Zullo, F.S.C., John Sinnwell, Robert Nelson, Betty Fairchild, Jeannine Gramick, Robert Nugent, Jim Bussen, Brian McNaught, Philip Scarpetta, Dennis Taylor, Steve Hogan, Anne McCaffrey, Michael Roccasalvo, Donald Greenbaum, Jeremiah Burmeister, and especially Steven Plane (not least for his assistance in preparing the typescript), and my brothers and sisters in St. Dominic who have distinguished themselves by their ministry to persons with AIDS — Lois McGovern, Timothy Radcliffe, Giles Hibbert, Gareth Moore, Michael Lopes, Donald Bramble, and Paul Colloton.

Richard Woods, O.P.
22 November 1987
Feast of Christ the King

NOTES

1. New York: Bantam Books ed., 1977, pp. 52-55.
2. Del Martin and Phyllis Lyon, *Lesbian/Woman*, New York: Bantam Books, 1972, pp. 74-83.
3. Ibid., see p. 134.
4. Notable examples include Sally Gearhart, "The Miracle of Lesbianism," in Sally Gearhart and William R. Johnson, eds., *Loving Women/Loving Men*, San Francisco: Glide Publications, 1974, pp. 118-52, "The Spiritual Dimension: Death and Resurrection of a Hallelujah Dyke," also by Sally Gearhart, in Ginny Vida, ed., *Our Right to Love: A Lesbian Resource Book*, Englewood Cliffs, NJ: Prentice-Hall, 1978, pp. 187-93. See also ibid., pp. 167-73, and especially *A Faith of Our Own*, Barbara Zanotti, ed., Trumansburg, NY: The Crossing Press, 1986.
5. Eileen Flynn, *AIDS: A Catholic Call for Compassion*, (Kansas City: Sheed and Ward, 1985), John Fortunato, *AIDS: The Spiritual Dilemma*, San Francisco: Harper and Row, 1987, and Vicky Costsick, ed., *AIDS: Meeting the Community Challenge* (Slough, England: St. Paul Publications, 1987). For a deeply spiritual but non-denominational approach to healing, also see the excellent resource manual by Tom O'Connor, with Ahmed Gonzalez-Nunez, *Living with AIDS: Reaching Out* (San Francisco: Corwin Publishers, 1987), especially pp. 42-64.

Prelude

PICKING up a book on sexuality was, not too long ago, a hazardous affair for the Catholic browser; thumbing through one on homosexuality required the sheerest nerve — unless, perhaps, one happened to be a priest. Times have changed. Sexuality is reasonably topical for Catholics. But, as you may know by now, it is still something of a challenge to tote a book on homosexuality to the sales counter without blushing, avoiding the salesperson's eyes, including it in a stack of other books (preferably biblical studies or psychology texts), or being a priest. Looking like a worried parent might help. Being gay might help, too.

Before 1969, "the love that dared not speak its name" was literally unmentionable in polite conversation. Following the Stonewall "riot" in New York City that year, gay liberation became a frequent theme in the literature and rhetoric of social and religious activism. Today, despite significant set-backs over the past few years — not least being the AIDS epidemic — gay liberation is still alive. Many gays and lesbians remain "out of the closet," proud to acknowledge who — and what — they are. Oppressive legal restrictions are still under attack by activists, an especially important concern in the wake of a flurry of anti-homosexual hysteria following the recognition of the serious problem AIDS presents to the heterosexual community as well as the gay world. Gay men and women are still interviewed on television and radio. Major films with homosexual themes are still shown in neighborhood theaters, on television, and on video-tape. And despite recent and strenuous counteroffensives, the movement for acceptance by the Church in the form of associations such as the Metropolitan Community Church, Dignity, Integrity, Lutherans Concerned, Evangelicals Concerned, and other church-related groups has continued. Clearly, however, the note of optimism so evident in the 'seventies and early 'eighties has been muted by the AIDS scare. Once again, many gay men and even lesbians find themselves jeopardized by their sexual orientation in the eyes of the state and the churches. Many are persecuted, directly or indirectly. Some are prosecuted. High judges proclaim that private, consensual sexual conduct by gays and lesbians is not protected under the U.S. Constitution or Bill of Rights. There are calls in Congress and state legislatures for quarantine and internment camps for those merely exposed to the AIDS virus.

It is no wonder that many homosexual men and women are once again troubled deeply by a sense of guilt or rejection, isolated from their families and religion, and cautious in the work place and community because of their sexuality. Not a few live in quiet but constant fear of exposure, ridicule, and condemnation.

This book is not so much about homosexuality as it is *for* homosexual men and women, especially those who are *not* "out." It is also for their relatives, friends, and associates — people who care about gays and lesbians, whether as teachers, pastors, counselors, co-workers, or just neighbors. It is also for the curious, ambivalent, fearful, and hostile — if only as a tender of hope and an invitation to care and compassion. It is not a technical theological study. Nor is it a book on the psychology or sociology of homosexuality, although I have not hesitated to plunder the sciences for information.

In the following pages, I approach homosexuality foremost as a fact rather than as a desirable or undesirable condition. Personally, I do not believe that a homosexual orientation as such constitutes individual or social pathology, whether physical, psychological, or spiritual. In pastoral and clinical practice, I have found that homosexual persons are as healthy (and unhealthy) as heterosexual persons, even given the greater social stress homosexual persons must endure daily.

Another Kind of Love is primarily an essay in spirituality — an offering of pastoral reflections and suggestions based on some six years' experience ministering directly to gay Catholics and other Christians and twenty years as a teacher of spirituality, a counselor, and a sexual dysfunction therapist. In order to provide a more concrete account of the situation of gay and lesbian Christians, I have incorporated some first-hand accounts supplied to me by students, clients, and friends. These narratives have been altered only to preserve anonymity. I also asked several gay men and lesbians as well as their relatives and friends to comment on certain subjects, which they have done far more knowledgeably and sensitively than I could have.

Writing (and re-writing) a book on homosexuality, like perusing or purchasing one, has its attendant risks. Working with gays and lesbians, as well as their parents, friends, children, and associates, has proved somewhat hazardous — doubts, misunderstandings, disagreements, strained relationships, impatience — all have played their possibly necessary role. But the benefits have been far greater. I am still only beginning to fathom, if only partially and superficially, the oppression and discrimination gay people experience in society and in church, every day of their lives, and often throughout a lifetime. I am still growing in my appreciation of the courage, humanity, and tenacious fidelity to the Church that characterize so many gay and lesbian Christians, as well as their great capacity for laughter, love, and sacrifice. Their gratitude for the little the Church has done in return continues to astonish and humble me.

It is my belief now, as it was my hope eighteen years ago, that the long-overdue ministry to homosexual persons is a mission of the Holy Spirit in our time, the success of which will bring the Church a major step forward on its way to true catholicism.

CHAPTER ONE

Living with Homosexuality

AS dusk fell over the chill city, men and women, singly, in couples, and small groups, approached the three-flat and disappeared into the late Victorian doorway behind the new brick wall and iron gate. Gathered in a third floor apartment, there were soon over forty people — some in their early twenties, a few three times that age, the rest around thirty-five or forty.

A few minutes later, a figure stepped into the center of the group, most of whom were seated on borrowed bridge chairs quietly conversing.

"Let's get started with a prayer, shall we?" The group fell silent.

"Heavenly Father," the man continued after a moment, "we have come here tonight to learn about the new rite of reconciliation...." The group, most of them Catholic, have assembled to watch a filmstrip on the sacrament of penance and share in a discussion which was followed by a short penance service. The speaker who led the opening prayer was a priest. Two other priests were present. I was one of them.

This gathering still reminds me of accounts of house church services among the early Christians. It took place in Chicago in Lent, 1976, but could have happened anywhere — Boston, Philadelphia, Detroit, or Los Angeles. It could almost have been 1986. The participants could have been members of almost any progressive parish in the country. Except for one circumstance. Most of them were gay.

A few blocks away, thousands of other gay men and women

were filling the bars and discos that catered to them, where they would dance, drink, meet friends, cruise for "tricks," or just watch the goings-on from the side.   Elsewhere, other men were looking for easy sex in steam baths or cruising the parks and beaches, "hustling trade" downtown, or loitering hopefully in bus and train depots, airports, and public lavatories, watching for a contact who was not a police decoy.   Still others probed through murky stores for pornographic magazines or viewed cheap films in arcades, or sat watching an endless chain of low-budget, scratchy films depicting activities that would stretch the imagination of an anatomist.

But the vast majority of gay women and men — some 20,000 of them — were settling in for an evening of leisure or boredom, whether alone or in couples, following the pattern of millions of their straight counterparts in the city and suburbs from whom they were otherwise indistinguishable.

Somewhere else in the city, a gay teenager, desperate and rejected, would attempt suicide.   Another was composing a prize-winning poem.   Yet another was shot trying to rob a liquor store, while some spent the night in prayer, reaching out in faith to all the others in their struggles, sufferings, and accomplishments.   Not a few were making sick calls, hearing confessions, or celebrating liturgical services.

HOMOSEXUAL

Most Americans over the age of thirty grew up with a strong conviction that gay was bad — an attitude characteristic of western civilization, and a feeling not unrelated to our dread of Blacks, Jews, Gypsies, other "foreigners," and our half-belief that "the only good Injun is a dead Injun."   Good, church-going Christians (above all) knew from the Bible that homosexuality was *heinous*.   We may not have been sure exactly what "heinous" meant, but it was evidently pretty terrible — and excluded "them" from the Kingdom of Heaven.   Or at least from the church, military service, and other respectable associations.

Before the late 1960s, "homosexuals" were hardly ever referred to directly, but as kids we knew about taking candy or accepting rides from strangers. For most of us, these attitudes continued through the elementary school years, when we learned jokes we hardly understood about "queers" and "fairies," eventually making the monumental discovery that there were *women* queers, too.

In high school and college, we may have even met "a" homosexual or two. We probably had suspicions about a few guys, especially the effeminate ones, and maybe even some of the tougher girls. But it was usually a fringe phenomenon — hovering uneasily at the far edges of consciousness except for the jokes and a few novels and perhaps an occasional magazine story or newspaper article. What we never suspected was that my friend in the next room, the basketball star, the spunky red-haired cheerleader who became a nun, the fat kid in architecture who used to laugh so hard at queer-jokes, the janitor, the dean, and the campus cop were all one of "them."

It is commonly held by social scientists that at least one out of every ten persons is predominantly homosexual. Gay knows no class differences, religious or ethnic barriers, socio-economic disparities, gender or age limits.[1] And if it were illegal to associate with "them," we'd all be in trouble.

For if you are not homosexual yourself, you *certainly* know someone who is. Among your friends and classmates, your co-workers, the doctors who have healed you, the clergy who have ministered to you, your teachers, and members of your family, some have been homosexual. Of course, in most cases you didn't know it, and probably don't now, because they were afraid to tell you. Afraid that you would reject them, perhaps injure them, have them fired or expelled, jailed, publicly disgraced, or otherwise victimized.

For the most part in our culture, people have considered gay men and lesbians to be sick, immoral, and predatory misfits worthy of neither pity nor pardon. They have been shunned, hounded, ridiculed, denounced from the pulpit and platform, and legislated against. Those convicted of sodomy and other felonious and "unspeakable crimes against God and nature" were often executed, even in recent times, or were given long prison sentences. Some men were "mercifully" allowed to submit to castration to escape decades of imprisonment. Others were forcibly emasculated. Blackmail is still a threat and sometimes an actual occurrence.

Two decades of social and legislative reform greatly mitigated the harshness of disapproval in European and American states. But in the last few years, the specter of AIDS has evoked a resurgence of threats and violence against homosexual persons in general, even though a very small minority of them will ever be exposed to the virus. I believe that these and the former attitudes and actions are far more dangerous and immoral than the "crimes" for which homosexual persons are targeted. However understandable such discrimination may have been in past ages, it was still inexcusable for any Christian or, for that matter, any civilized person. It is far more so today. Quite simply, I am convinced that the "traditional" civil and religious prejudice against homosexuality, based as it was largely on ignorance, fear, and fantasy, is to that extent now untenable. It is ungodly, inhuman, and destructive of individual rights and dignity as well as of the common welfare.

I am further convinced that, as a human condition, homosexuality should not be (as it increasingly *is* not) considered a disease, personal defect, or an emotional disorder in itself. Hence, it is incorrect, misleading, and degrading to speak of homosexuality as "curable." It is no less wrong for religious people to label homosexuality a curse, an affliction, or a depravity. Nor should all homosexual behavior be indiscriminately condemned in advance as invariably and gravely sinful without much further and more careful study of scripture as well as the many varieties of homosexual experience, attitudes, and activities. Similarly, criminal penalties for private sexual acts between consenting adults of any sexual orientation should be abolished. Placing ordinary men and women in the same category as rapists, child-molesters, prostitutes, and pimps is an injustice no sane society should tolerate, much less the grossly inequitable enforcement of laws frequently practiced by the police and courts, in addition to entrapment, espionage, and harassment. More positively, I am also convinced that homosexual women and men can and do live with freedom and dignity as creative members of society and worthy members of the Church. (Although speaking from a Christian viewpoint and mainly with Catholics in mind, most of what I have to say about the religious situation is, I hope, applicable within the Jewish and Islamic traditions, which share the same biblical heritage.) The *fact* is that most gay persons are responsible, dedicated citizens as well as honest, committed church-goers — just like the rest of the population, a fact borne out by another fact: most homosexual men and women are "invisible." They cannot be distinguished from the population at large except by their own admission. Yet these same women and men must endure perpetual tension. They *know* that they are different in the one respect that, in the somewhat warped mentality of western peoples, will overshadow all the rest. (While a universal human phenomenon, homosexuality has been viewed in a variety of ways by Asian, African, Native American, Polynesian and other non-western peoples, often with comparatively remarkable tolerance.)

Living with homosexuality means living with a difference. Doing so well requires developing personal resources and reserves of psychic energy few straight people are ever forced to drawn on or cultivate. For this reasons, one study concluded that from a psychological perspective the "healthy homosexual" is probably *healthier* than the great majority of heterosexual people who, confronted even occasionally by the challenges and conflicts a gay person ordinarily faces daily, would crumble psychologically.[2]

Fortunately, most gays and lesbians possess sufficient stamina to survive the stresses they continually encounter. Sometimes this strength rises to the surface of their personalities, and they become hard and bitter — but not often, as far as I can tell, and certainly less so than in the case of tightly closeted homosexual men and women. Sometimes the most vulnerable areas of gays' and lesbians' inner selves are walled off by defensive or evasive attitudes and behavior — but not too frequently. As a result, they manage to acquire an assortment of psychic scars, but they are rarely disfigured.

Their courageous, flippant, sometimes brazen approach to the "harsh realities" of life reminds me sometimes of the classic circus clown — not the shallow goofiness of Bozo or the commercial antics of Ronald McDonald, but the Chaplinesque quality of an Emmet Kelly, or the great comic-tragic figures of legend — Till Eulenspiegel, Scaramouche, Mattachine, Harlequin — whose attitude affirmed, even in blood, the value of living as humanly as possible in a world infected by radical evil. Their secret is courage, love, and laughter, an urgent will to savor the goodness of life in a real and carefree celebration whenever the opportunity can be made to arise.

Perhaps that is why they have always been called *gay*. In any event, there is a clue here worth considering from a different viewpoint: that of the religious questioner, who in scouring for meaning in human life, ought to be alerted by the aura of the mystic and prophet whenever the clowns come in. Or out.

We shall return to the clowns later on. Here, to begin with, it will be helpful to look briefly at the nature of human sexuality from an empirical viewpoint in order to grasp something later on of the spiritual meaning and value of homosexuality.

THE FOURTEEN SEXES

Biologically, the division of the human race into male and female genders is adequate but by no means perfect. Sexuality is not defined solely by the presence of external sex organs or the functions of begetting, conceiving, and bearing offspring, although the specific attributes of the two genders constitute sufficient and necessary criteria to account for fundamentals such as procreation. Considered by itself, however, such a basis of comparison remains purely physical. It even fails to take into account the associated elements of mate selection, homemaking, and child-rearing practices. Actually, sexuality is the complex product of at least seven interconnected physiological, psychological, and sociological systems, all differently experienced by males and females, even in the case of the higher, sub-human mammals. Humanly speaking, there are also specifically spiritual elements involved — ethics, religious values, aesthetics, and above all, or underlying all, intelligence and love.

Structurally, *biological* maleness and femaleness are designations resulting from a complex of five elements: chromosomes, the endocrine system, hormones, the internal sex organs, and, finally, the external sex organs. But viewed dynamically, sexual development is a process that spans the temporal spread of a life, beginning with the genetic programming that occurs even before conception and continues through the embryological period, during which each human person-in-becoming undergoes many structural changes, including for males the transformation of rudimentary female sex organs into male ones. After birth, the process accompanies further organization and growth of the brain and nervous system, climaxing in much later changes produced by glandular maturation at puberty. Physiological development proceeds along male-female lines through adulthood, menopause, and the male climacteric, and culminates in senescence.

Individually, sexuality is constituted only partially by biological development. Also crucially important is the correlative *psycho-social* process of sexual individuation, from the diffuse experiences of the new-born infant through several intermediate stages leading to eventual maturity. During this process of consciousness-formation, the two psychological elements of sexuality are established: gender *roles* are socially communicated along lines culturally associated with gender *identity*. That is, one's sense of masculinity or femininity (role) is not identical with but relative to experienced maleness or femaleness (identity) — the gender "assigned" one at birth and reinforced during rearing.

Sexual "orientation" or "object-preference" seems to be an expression of gender identity, but it is by no means equivalent. In effect, heterosexuality and homosexuality (and the various shades between) encompass a range of possible occasions for sexual arousal; they do not *constitute* gender identity.

A person's gender identity (that is, the awareness of being a male or female) is generally considered to be at the threshold of fixity by the age of eighteen months. By forty-eight months, identity is normally permanent. Acquiring culturally appropriate gender roles continues for years, however. One *learns* how to be a boy, a woman, a father, or even a grandmother in a cultural and social setting. Such roles are not simply given in the order of things as if by magic — although it may seem so at times.

Because sexuality is the overall product of a series of complex interactions of various biological, psychological, and social systems, it has a homeostatic and approximative character. That is, sexuality is a process of many factors *balanced* in a *more or less* specific proportion. Even the ancients knew that nature is only generally constant and predictable: natural factors are *normative*, not exact. Variations *always* surround the nucleus of a general type of natural phenomenon. Sexual development, too, is more or less determinate; normally, greater or lesser variations can occur at any point from parental genetic endowment to the last moments of a person's life.

Some effects of sexual developmental variations will be minor, others will be drastic. Thus, some persons are born hermaphroditic (retaining vestigial organs of the opposite sex), or perhaps who will be sterile, or whose hormonal balance will be different, or whose sex chromosomes will exceed or lack the normal pair. Occasionally a child is assigned the wrong gender at birth because of small male or large female sex organs and is reared as a member of the opposite sex. Other children may be assigned the correct identity, but somehow acquire some of the role characteristics of the opposite gender, resulting in male effeminacy or female masculinity. Sexual orientation, even in such cases, is not a function of physiology, gender identification, or role characteristics. Although there is growing evidence that certain elements of sexual orientation may have a pre-natal hormonal basis, the scientific community still inclines to the belief that sexual preference is a learned response acquired at a very early age.[3]

Later sexual attitudes and behavior are at least as variable as the many factors that influence early physiological and psychological sexuality. The way in which an infant is reared, such as the intimacy with which he or she is handled by both mother and father, will have enormous sexual repercussions in adolescence and adulthood. Puberty is an especially critical period of emerging self-definition. So is menopause or the male climacteric, but in different respects for women and men.

Because of the complexities of sexual development, it is not surprising that the social aspect of sexual orientation — who will be a desirable sexual partner — allows for considerable flexibility. The predominant pattern has always been heterosexual — males and females will be primarily attracted to each other sexually, but hardly to *every* member of the opposite gender. Our particular preferences are, like all matters of "taste," personal and characteristic.

The biological, indeed evolutionary, significance of dominant heterosexuality is obvious. But given the apparent "bisexuality" of as much as eighty percent of the population (as determined by Kinsey and others over three decades of research),[4] that is, the capacity under certain conditions of being sexually aroused by certain members of either gender, it has become increasingly questionable scientifically whether homosexuality and bisexuality fall outside the *normal* range of variation. (It should be borne in mind that the concept of "normal" is used differently in science, religious discourse, and ordinary conversation.)

Some element of homosexuality seems to be a component factor in virtually all sexual development and behavior in two ways. First, masculinity and femininity as real, complementary psychological characteristics are part of everyone's potential identity and character, just as (and possibly because) both male and female hormones are present in both women and men. Similarly, male sexual organs are in fact specialized forms of common embryological organs which, without the presence of male hormones, would always develop into female organs. That is why men have nipples and a vestigial uterus in the lining of the urethra and why women have a clitoris, which is not a vestigial penis, but an organically predeveloped one. (The nipples of male babies sometimes lactate, an often startling but harmless occurrence.)

Such physical "bisexuality," with its correlative psychological resonance (sometimes called "androgyny"), enables us to be whole persons, capable of relating to members of both genders. They constitute necessary qualities for a balanced human personality. Developmentally, we incorporate personality traits of *both* our parents (or of other model male and female adults), features which are not only the basis for being able to relate to members of both genders socially, but are themselves part of our fundamental make-up physically and spiritually. Ordinarily, one aspect of gender role-potential (like hormone balance) will predominate, the other recede. Both, however, seem necessary for wholeness. Stifling either of these complementary sexual aspects of our personalities produces tension, fragmentation, and often pathological states of mind and behavior analogous to a deficiency or excess in hormonal balance, such as fear and hatred of the opposite gender (misanthropy or misogyny).

The second homosexual (or bisexual) personality component is attraction at some period in life to members of the same gender instead of (or as well as) the opposite one — an attraction that is a *normal* part of the maturation process, but which may never find expression in direct genital activity. Studies indicate, however, that the majority of males and many females in America and Europe have had some kind of homosexual experience some time in their lives, usually a youthful experiment. There is no reason to believe that all such isolated experiences are dangerous, evil, or sick. Presumably, they perform an often important function in the creation of sexual identity. Further, there is no compelling evidence that such passing episodes can "reorient" a basically heterosexual person towards exclusive or even predominant homosexuality.

True homosexual persons differ from heterosexual persons mainly in that they prefer members of the same gender as the exclusive or predominant "object" of sexual desire during most of their lives. As many as sixty percent of homosexual persons are not exclusively so oriented, however. Like the predominantly heterosexual population, they can be considered more or less bisexual.

Some homosexuality undoubtedly involves a deep, probably unconscious fear of the opposite sex. It may well stem from a profound sense of sexual inadequacy, or both of these. But such instances of neurotic development do not apply to all cases of homosexuality, and decidedly not to most. Very many homosexual men and women are in this respect clearly healthy.[5]

From animal studies, it seems evident that in every group of higher mammals, there is a wide range of normal sexual behavior rather than a single type, including at least partial homosexuality.[6] Long-term, exclusive homosexual preference, however, seems to be a purely human phenomenon. It is certainly true that some homosexual preference and activity has been an aspect of the human condition from the very start of things and (as far as we know) in every land and culture. Attitudes toward homosexuality or bisexuality, as well as the treatment of homosexual and bisexual persons, have varied enormously from culture to culture. But the incidence of both is apparently fairly constant statistically.

To suggest, on the other hand, that homosexual preference and activity may be biologically and sociologically within the normal range of behavior is *not* to say that there are no abnormal homosexual conditions, or that homosexual persons do not suffer serious problems. Normality in this respect depends not only upon the persistence of the variation and the margin of variability. In addition, the variation (or "deviation" in sociological jargon) must not be destructive to the individual or to society. The case for judging the empirical normality of homosexuality and other sexual variations thus depends upon both its status as a statistically constant factor as well as its non-pathological character.

INCIDENCE AND PATHOLOGY

No one knows for certain just how many persons in any given population are in fact homosexual, since for the most part homosexual men and women are indistinguishable from anyone else. In addition, many wish to keep their orientation secret. Reliable sources continue to estimate the number of *exclusive* homosexual persons at four percent. (The number of *exclusive* heterosexual persons is also estimated to be about four percent.) The number of persons who have had *some* homosexual experience, however fleeting, in their lives is much higher, well over fifty percent. But less than a majority of men and women have actually experienced significant genital relations with persons of the same sex. Thus researchers place the number of *predominant and exclusive* homosexual persons at about ten percent.[7] That true bisexuality is much more prevalent than once considered has been demonstrated with tragic consequences in the spread of AIDS within the heterosexual population through bisexual contact.

Few students of human sexuality doubt or deny the overall statistical constancy of homosexuality and bisexuality. The real debate concerns the issue of pathology: are these forms of human sexual preference socially or individually harmful?

Since the late nineteenth century, medical and scientific thinking has shifted from a position maintaining that homosexuality is a disease or a disorder to one of tolerance or neutrality and in many cases of acceptance as a normal variation. That is to say, homosexuality as such is not pathological. Similarly, and largely as a consequence, in most nations of the world and many states in America, homosexual relations between consenting adults are no longer considered to be criminal acts. Theologians and church leaders have been much slower in declassifying homosexuality as evil and sinful, but there is a trend in that direction as well.[8] If it seems conclusive to a majority of medical and scientific researchers that homosexuality is not an aberration, a disease, or a threat, but represents a constant, sizable phenomenon in virtually all societies, it would also seem reasonable to conclude that homosexual orientation and some forms of behavior constitute a normal and natural part of the order of the world from a religious perspective. There are, of course, some instances of homosexual attitudes and conduct that *are* clearly disordered, criminal, and sinful — just as there are with respect to heterosexuality. The point is that such instances do not typify the majority of cases among either group.

Trends to the contrary notwithstanding, many psychologists still consider homosexuality a disorder, a curable problem akin to alcoholism or various phobias. Several nations, notably Russia and East Germany, and most states in America still penalize homosexual conduct severely. Many churches anathematize homosexual persons, refuse to license homosexual ministers, and many, perhaps most, Christian theologians still consider all forms of homosexual activity to be gravely sinful, even if they look on homosexual orientation itself as "an objective disorder," a misfortune, or as a morally neutral condition.[9] The debate will surely continue for some time to come.

NOTES

1. The word "gay" is often used synonymously with *homosexual*, but there are significant differences between the two terms. *Homosexual* signifies sexual attraction towards members of one's own gender, whether or not it is expressed in overt behavior or even consciously recognized. *Gay* is an older, narrower term, referring primarily to the awareness and acceptance of homosexual orientation and, to some extent, sharing that awareness with others, that is, being "out of the closet." (See below, p. 90.) Gay consciousness also includes a wide range of personal and social sensibilities differing in certain respects from those of heterosexual ("straight") persons. In this sense, *gay* need not connote overt genital activity.

2. Cf. Mark Freedman, "Far from Illness: Homosexuals May Be Healthier than Straights," *Psychology Today* 8, 10 (March, 1975): 27-33. Cf. Evelyn Hooker, "The Adjustment of the Male Overt Homosexual," *Journal of Projective Techniques* 21 (March 1957): 30: "Homosexuality may be a deviation in sexual pattern which

is within the normal range, psychologically." See also George Weinberg, *Society and the Healthy Homosexual*, Garden City, NY: Doubleday Anchor Books, 1973, and below, p. 27.

3. For a recent discussion of these issues, see Elizabeth Moberly, *Psychogenesis: The Early Development of Gender Identity*, London: Routledge and Kegan Paul, 1983.

4. Cf. Alfred Kinsey, et al., *Sexual Behavior in the Human Male*, Philadelphia: W. B. Saunders, 1948, and *Sexual Behavior in the Human Female*, Philadelphia: W. B. Saunders, 1953. Kinsey's pioneering work, although challenged, has remained the basis for all subsequent research in the demography of homosexuality. For a recent discussion of related issues, see Benjamin Sadock et al., eds., *The Sexual Experience*, Baltimore: Williams and Wilkins Co., 1976, and Judd Marmor, ed., *Homosexual Behavior: A Modern Reappraisal*, New York: Basic Books, Inc., 1980.

5. Cf. Freedman, art. cit. See also the Resources for Further Reading, pp. 181ff.

6. Cf. Cllelan S. Ford and Frank A. Beach, *Patterns of Sexual Behavior*, New York: Harper and Row, 1972, pp. 134-43. See also Arno Karlen, *Sexuality and Homosexuality: A New View*, New York: W.W. Norton and Co., Inc., pp. 399-434, and R. Denniston, "Ambisexuality in Animals," in Marmor, ed. cit., pp. 25-40.

7. These figures reflect the cumulative findings of the Institute for Sex Research, Indiana University. For discussion, see Wainwright Churchill, *Homosexual Behavior among Males*, Englewood Cliffs, NJ: Prentice-Hall, 1971, pp. 50-52. Cf. also Karlen, op. cit., pp. 442-55, and Marmor, ed. cit., pp. 6-7.

8. Although the range of opinion and reasoning varies, among Catholic theologians who have adopted a more tolerant viewpoint toward homosexuality are Gregory Baum, Lisa Sowle Cahill, Charles Curran, John Dedek, Philip Keane, Anthony Kosnick, Daniel Maguire, Richard McCormick, John Giles Milhaven, and Vincent Rush. In this regard see especially "An Introduction to the Pastoral Care of Homosexual People," Catholic Social Welfare Commission, Catholic Bishops of England and Wales (1980), Mt. Rainier, MD: New Ways Ministry, 1981. Many Episcopalian and protestant theologians have also accepted the relative normalcy of homosexuality from a moral viewpoint, including Norman Pittenger, Letha Scanzoni, and Virginia Ramey Mollencott. See Resources for Further Reading below, pp. 181ff.

9. The official position of the Roman Catholic Church, that although homosexual orientation is not in itself either sinful or evil, the genital expression of that orientation is objectively sinful, was most recently reiterated in the "Letter on the Pastoral Care of Homosexual Persons," issued by Cardinal Joseph Ratzinger for the Congregation for the Doctrine of the Faith (1 October 1986). A compendium of authoritative statements from Catholic bishops and theologians reflecting a wider range of positions, *Homosexuality and the Magisterium: Documents from the Vatican and the U.S. Bishops 1975-1985*, ed. by John Gallagher (1986) is available from New Ways Ministry, Mt. Rainier, MD. See also "A Time to Speak: A Collection of Contemporary Statements from U.S. Catholic Sources on Homosexuality, Gay Ministry, and Social Justice," Robert Nugent, SDS, and Jeannine Gramick, SSND, eds., Mt. Rainier, MD: New Ways Ministry, 1982. A very balanced position on the moral issues as well as a compassionate pastoral message can be found in the statement of the Bishops of England and Wales, "An Introduction to the Pastoral Care of Homosexual People," cited above.

CHAPTER TWO

The Mystery of Homosexuality

DESPITE the growing amount of information about homosexuality, no one really knows how it comes about. Most "definitive" explanations explain too much or too little; one hypothesis accounts for a few "cases" (usually those it is founded upon), but no known theory can explain the facts in the great majority of them. Cultural differences appear to be more rather than less significant than was previously thought; patterns differ enormously from place to place and from one period of time to another. Published psychological theories directly contradict each other. The experts continue to disagree.[1]

What seems clear is that homosexuality is not traceable to a single cause or even to a typical pattern of causes; any number of factors may be involved in each personal history. Moreover, homosexuality is not an "all or nothing" state, but a tendency which is more or less predominant in all normal people, as well as one which varies in importance and strength, especially during the early phases of psychological development. Conscious homosexual interest may be a transient stage in a person's life. It may well emerge late in life even after decades of "dormancy." But generally, the dominant pattern is set early in life. Consequently, when expressed in behavior homosexuality is a highly variable phenomenon. It would be more accurate on the whole to speak of "homosexualities" rather than homosexuality, given the range of differences in origin and expression.[2]

Further, important differences between male and female gay

experience are becoming increasingly clear as lesbians speak out, write more, and receive greater attention from researchers. "Gay" hardly covers the full range of male homosexuality, much less that of women. But "lesbian" itself is similarly inadequate, given the spectrum of attitudes, backgrounds, lifestyles, and situations gay women experience.[3]

ORIGIN AND MYSTERY

Notwithstanding the occasional claims to the contrary (those made by East German endocrinologist Gunter Dörner being perhaps the most recent[4]), it seems evident in the vast majority of instances that, as discussed in chapter one, homosexual preference is not strictly innate, that is, a condition rooted in the physiological make-up of a person, but is rather a behavioral expression of gender identity acquired at an early age as a disposition which is confirmed by later experience — just as in the case of heterosexual orientation. But so early does this orientation begin, and so strong is its direction, however unconscious at first, that it *becomes* practically equivalent to an innate personality structure. Such "constitutive" or "constitutional" homosexuality appears to be only minimally subject to later modification, just as in the case of constitutional heterosexual preference.

It seems to me that even if the psycho-physiological and socio-cultural origins (or "causes") of the varieties of homosexual orientation are one day discovered and techniques for altering sexual preference are perfected, homosexuality will still remain a mystery. For, as the Catholic philosopher Gabriel Marcel might have said, it is not a puzzle to be solved in the laboratory or the psychiatrist's office, but a human situation which men and women find themselves already involved in, one which they must address and live with.

Thus, to those for whom homosexual preference is the dominant and most continuous direction of "object choice," homosexuality is an existential "given" that can be accepted or rejected, but not "cured." The equation of homosexual feelings and experience with sickness or evil is a barbarism we are all better off relegating to the moralistic, magical medicine of past ages. According to the American Psychiatric Association, the American Psychological Association, and the National Institute of Mental Health, homosexuality is not in itself to be considered a disease. Similarly, from a religious perspective, speaking of "healing" people of homosexuality is an abuse of language and persons, as the bishops of England and Wales recognized in their pastoral statement, "An Introduction to the Pastoral Care of Homosexual People" (1979): "In the case of true homosexuals or 'inverts,' professional therapy may be helpful to assist them in accepting their condition positively, but therapy should never be suggested in a way that raises false expectations of a reverse or modification of the homosexual condition."[5]

Like everyone else, gay people sometimes have problems, often serious ones, about sexuality, whether these stem from their own or other peoples' attitudes and behavior. Gays also have problems that are distinct from their sexual orientation and its consequences. But most are not problem-ridden neurotics (at least no more so than anyone else!), and to define *them* as a problem because of their sexual preference is the opposite of helping. To cite again the Catholic Bishops of England and Wales, "It is incorrect to claim that homosexuals have a high incidence of mental disorder. This is simply not borne out by research."[6]

Over six years of ministering to the gay community and five more years as a therapist have led me to believe that, despite many "common" problems and difficulties, as well as those more typical of homosexual persons, gay men and women are generally ordinary, well-adjusted people who approach life with courage and — importantly — with success. Their stories, and those of their relatives, friends and associates, are an important part of the mystery of human sexuality — much more important, I feel, than the stereotyped but unrepresentative accounts of disturbed gays that fill the pages of so many books written by those whose professional competence lies in treating sickness.

Because the origin and persistence of homosexuality remains mysterious in each person's life as well as collectively, searching for its meaning and purpose becomes a profound challenge to many gays, often providing the dominant context of their relationship with God. One young man wrote to me: "I always hated God for making me a homosexual. After all, he's omnipotent and could do all or everything. Therefore, he could have made me straight. But I've lately felt there must have been a reason, but God only knows why."

As we shall see later on, the religious moment of faith for many gay men and women often comes as a meaning-giving experience of acceptance from a source beyond themselves. Others, hurt and confused by the mystery of their situation as well as by the rejection of those closest to them, turn to God in their need: "At the start I didn't really feel any change. To me being gay and Catholic were completely compatible. But in high school, as more and more of my friends became interested in girls and I had no such feelings, I turned to God more often as my concern increased. You might say that I used Him as a shoulder to cry on." The Christian response to the mystery of homosexuality does lie, I think, in attempting to see the situation of gay men and women in the context of God's purposes — although what those plans are, we may never know. And although both individual and social destiny must remain to some extent enshrouded in mystery and thus an occasion for faith and hope, I think it is possible to discern something of the meaning of homosexuality in a religious sense — not completely, but more as a hint or a suggestion. That, however, must wait for a later chapter.

LESBIANISM

Lesbian experience is possibly even more highly variegated and thus more mysterious than male gay experience. Many women, perhaps the majority of lesbians, come to maturity lacking any sexual interest in men and gravitate naturally to gay relationships. Others identify themselves as lesbian for reasons far different from sexual orientation alone. As with a surprisingly large number of gay men, many come out after years of heterosexual marriage, often being mothers of children. Having been patronized, restricted, emotionally and perhaps even physically abused by their husbands, these women seek the company of those who can most easily understand and support them, either for a time or permanently. In some cases, such women are not looking for sex at all and in fact can be called homosexual only in a limited sense.

As noted elsewhere in this book, *pseudohomosexuality*, a term coined by Dr. Lionel Ovesey, has been used almost exclusively to refer to men who resort to homosexual behavior in order to cope with unconscious needs for power or dependency.[7] Similarly, many women who adopt a homosexual life-style because of problems or difficulties, perhaps irreversible ones, are not truly homosexual, for physical experience is not the real goal of their relationships. They can be called lesbian or gay, however, because of the emotional fulfillment they seek and often find in same-sex relationships. Such relationships need not be considered compensation in a pathological sense, for they may well represent a positive adjustment, that is, one which significantly reduces anxiety.

Further, many heterosexual women who have experienced difficulty in married life seek out the companionship of gay men to find the kind of non-threatening masculinity they desire, either provisionally or indefinitely.[8] While these women should not be called lesbian, they could probably be considered gay since they associate with gay men and inhabit a niche in the gay world. (Calling them "fag-hags" or "fruit flies" is abusive, despite the emotional dependency some may manifest. For openly ridiculing such women while allowing them freely to associate in gay men's haunts is merely another incursion of the macho mystique into the gay world. Tagging someone a "fag-hag" implicitly degrades gay men themselves as it demeans the women they so label.)   Like their counterparts, lesbians may fear, hate, tolerate or like and even love members of the opposite sex — both gay and straight. But they prefer their own sex. Being aware of and accepting themselves as gay is what lesbian means. It is much more than sexual orientation or even being "out." Nor is lesbianism "a matter of gender-role designation, but contains within it elements of psychological, emotional and spiritual involvement...."[9] Part of the spiritual involvement in lesbianism is a social consciousness, a sense of belonging to a vast sisterhood whose immediate destiny is closely linked with women's liberation throughout the world. In many respects, lesbianism can be described more accurately as an emotional and spiritual solidarity in which overt sexual behavior has a real but more subsidiary value than it does for male gays, for whom emotional companionship and political solidarity are generally of less immediate importance.

Among male gays, too, sexual gratification alone is generally overrated as the prime factor in relationships — both long- and short-term. That is, there are usually deeper motives involved in forming a gay relationship, including symbolic values. While many lovers have told me that were it not for the physical relationship, they would not likely even be friends, I know of many gay couples who remain faithfully together but who have no common sex life — or very little — because of age, accident, or other physical or psychological dispositions.

The fundamental psycho-physiological and sociological differences between the sexes are more operative in the divergence between male and lesbian relationships, I think, than the more particular differences between lesbians and gay males as gay. Importantly, gays of both sexes have proved themselves capable of transcending these differences by means of motives other than psycho-physical attraction alone. I am referring to the specifically human and therefore spiritual values of care, fidelity, trust, and commitment. But the fundamental differences between male and female sexuality make it more difficult for gays than for straights to appreciate each other's values and life-styles.

Thus the "nesting" or domestic proclivities of lesbians, in contrast to the more restless and public behavior of male gays, owes something to their fundamental femaleness, just as the excursions of gay men have a real psycho-physiological basis. Strict segregation of the sexes in the gay world extenuates these fundamental traits to the point of caricature. There is cause, therefore, to welcome greater contact among lesbians and male gays, and some evidence that such affectionate association is increasing, along with greater mutual understanding and appreciation.

LIVING GAILY

Human sexuality, as should be obvious by now, is complex, variable, and developmental. Heterosexuality, while the dominant direction of genital interest in human persons, is not sharply defined, but exists as a disposition more or less conjoined with the capacity for (and perhaps the expression of) homosexual interest in all but a small fraction of the male and female population.

Suppressing one's homosexual capacities is destructive of integral personhood just as is suppressing one's heterosexual capacities. As the foundation for friendships between members of the same sex, these capacities must be cultivated and carefully integrated into the overall pattern of life experiences. This is *not* to say that genital homosexual or heterosexual activities should be casually or deliberately engineered "in order to find out what it's all about." Sexual experimentation, while perhaps tolerable in adolescent behavior, is most likely immature and depersonalizing for adults.

In fact, the great majority of men and women are simply not "turned on" for the most part by the prospect of genital intimacy with someone of the same sex — or in the case of homosexual persons, the opposite sex. Nevertheless, "bisexuality" as the human capacity for love and affection, that is, friendship, for both men and women is a necessary component of full human development. (It is important to bear in mind that if, at some moment in a person's life, this "bisexual" capacity is expressed in terms of genital experience, that does not constitute the person "a" bisexual any more than an isolated homosexual or heterosexual encounter makes someone "a" homosexual or "a" heterosexual.[10])

The suppression of bisexual capacities occurs either by avoiding the company of men or women, usually because of sexual fears, or by stifling any realization of affection for those unavoidably encountered in the course of business, recreation, worship, etc. Bereft of the human dimension of affectivity, such relationships, although common to both gay and straight people, are harmful to individual growth and social well-being. Human associations are turned into mechanical affairs of utility or convenience, possibly of mutual, but superficial, enjoyment. Real affection, lasting concern, and intimacy are precluded from the outset. The loss of potential richness and creativity in such experiences is incalculable.

Gay advocates and psychologists have coined the term "homophobia" to refer to the unhealthy state of fear, aversion and hatred many, perhaps most, straight persons feel when they encounter or even think about homosexuality, whether in themselves or others. There is a complementary attitude that is just as crippling and objectionable among gays, however; it might as well be called "heterophobia" — the unreasonable fear of the opposite sex, usually associated, as in the case of homophobia, with repulsive fantasies of genitals or sexual intercourse. Both of these irrational attitudes may be converted into expressions that are sexist and demeaning, whether directed at all gays (or straights), or at males or females of either sexual orientation. Thus arises, for instance, the more or less voluntary segregation of gay men and lesbians within gay institutions and activities. The sad and debilitating moral diseases traditionally given long Greek names, *misogyny* and *misanthropy*, know no barriers of race, creed, color, *or* sexual preference.

Several positive attitudes can be singled out as particularly important with regard to living creatively as or with a gay person, and I wish here to devote some discussion to them.

ACCEPTANCE

Living with homosexuality involves, first of all, affirmation: accepting yourself, if you are gay — or accepting your friend, relative, or associate. Acceptance here does not mean mere resignation to the inescapable — "nothing more can be done," nor does it mean "bearing one's cross," a burden, trial, or temptation, much less a punishment for God knows what infraction of the celestial rules. Rather, acceptance means an affirmation of yourself or someone else "as is," a decision which demands an end to resentment, self-dissection, worry, and doubt. Acceptance means saying yes to what we all genuinely are, faults included, but not to the myths, stereotypes, and fantasies which distort our perceptions and rule our expectations of what we and others should be.

Such affirmation is sometimes — if wrongly — called "self-forgiveness," wrongly because there is no sin in being homosexual, and thus nothing to forgive. (But if ending years of self-recrimination, regret, envy, and anger is called "self-forgiveness," I would certainly not object strongly.) Whatever it is called, self-acceptance will very likely be the first and principal element in any gay spirituality. It is an act of faith, love, and hope — not only in oneself, but in God, from whom all acceptance, affirmation, *and* forgiveness come (mainly through other people). Spirituality is the way in which we live out that faith, hope, and love, particularly with regard to those around us, who very often need — and deserve — our forgiveness and acceptance, as we need theirs. All true forgiveness is a form of exchange; we receive as we give.

Affirming your own worth — or another's — in the midst of a world that continually declares your worthlessness as vile, dangerous, and sick, is hardly easy. But it can be done — by refusing to acquiesce in the world's verdict, and by resolutely cultivating the positive talents, qualities, skills, and capacities you are gifted with in whatever degree.

LIBERATION

The greatest enemy of self-acceptance is probably a sense of guilt merely for being what you are. Such guilt, however, is rarely a personal reaction to wrong freely done, but the internalization of society's disparagement: an impersonal and unjust rejection communicated by a thousand gross and subtle means.

Thus, acquittal does not usually come by means of some act of "self-forgiveness" or even a change in social norms, but by the realization that such norms are not only relative, but frequently wrong. Liberation from social guilt results from a deliberate disengagement from society's totalitarian claims, not in the form of complete anarchy, but more as a mode of detachment in the religious sense — "letting go," as Meister Eckhart would have said. The independence many gays achieve by choosing to live by their own freely chosen values not only provides them with a measure of social autonomy that makes for psychological health, but it also contributes *to* society, for gays thus acquire a keen critical sense. They have learned about the emperor's new clothes... and don't hesitate to say so.

Many gays' deep sense of personal guilt often has a religious quality about it, a feeling of damnation. Again, this is often "merely" the inner version of what parents and churchmen preach at them, a condemnation reiterated in many ways in daily life. Again, too, such judgments are impersonal and arbitrary, netting all and sundry in the generalizations of self-righteousness. *God* surely does not curse anyone "from his mother's womb." Consequently, forgiveness is both assured and sorely needed if gay men and lesbians are to become truly free of a legacy of past hurts and injustices.

I shall have more to say later about the place of religion and spirituality in gay life. Here, I wish only to note that by accepting homosexuality as a component of their personalities, gays and lesbians can also accept it "graciously" as part of the divine design for human existence. By so doing, they can recognize their sexuality — their humanly ordinary but vast capacity to give and receive love — as an occasion for personal growth and sanctity, that is, the wholeness that flows from authentic spirituality.

Only by denying and rejecting so intimate a dimension of their personality can their homosexuality become for gays a curse, an obstacle to happiness and an excuse for failing to make the most out of life. Bitterness, resentment, and misery must follow, or — at best — the needless excision of part of themselves as the terrible price paid in the belief that such mutilation is necessary for entry into the Kingdom of Heaven. This kind of self-destruction is not only unnecessary, and far from what Jesus meant in his parable, but sinful. It produces not saints, but psychological and spiritual cripples.

For parents, friends, and associates such as teachers and pastors, learning to accept homosexuality means that they should no more blame themselves for the orientation of someone they care for and may have been responsible for, than they should blame him or her. It is not a question at all of blame, failure, or retribution, not even of cure, but rather of affirming a fact about a person who deserves and probably desperately needs love and support at a critical moment in life. Accepting a gay person does not mean approving everything gay. It merely means recognizing that she or he is a valuable, lovable, and vulnerable person for whom life will have sufficient pain without the added burden of rejection.

When young persons, in trust and hope, reach out and confide in someone they esteem that they are gay, a response of grief, anger, or denial can effect almost irreparable harm.[11] The young, however, have no monopoly on sensitivity and vulnerability; it can take far greater courage for adults to reveal themselves to a cherished friend, parent, or, indeed, a spouse or children, for the risk of rejection can be far more threatening. Humiliation can be complete and final; public exposure can bring lasting ruin.

Like true forgiveness, self-acceptance must eventually find its ground and validation in acceptance by others. The radical self-acceptance which constitutes an act of faith in life's meaning and value even when rejected by friends, family, and acquaintances can only rise from a more fundamental Source, whose acceptance is absolute and unconditional. As we have already seen, for some gays faith in God often coincides with self-acceptance in just this way — being accepted not *despite* what they are, but *for* what they are and what they can become. The deep reassurance that they are loved enables them in turn to share that acceptance with others. One young woman of twenty-nine put it thus: "My feelings toward God have something to do with how I feel that He feels about me; and, consequently, how I feel about myself. As my self-esteem increases, I find that I am better able to be responsive to God and to others."

Acceptance, then, rests upon compassion as well as affirmation. It finds expression in thanksgiving and celebration. As someone expressed it: "My homosexuality has not in any way affected my appreciation, devotion, or love for God. Since the age of 12, when I first realized my sex-role, I have continually thanked God for making me what I am — first and foremost, one of His creatures... providentially made to live as I am in this age of history, and secondarily, a gay person. I had no choice in being born gay or hetero; rather, I was given my human nature and 'beingness' from the Being of all beings! I sincerely feel that we have to accept what and who we are, and accept it with our hearts... never feeling different from others, but rather as being part of Divine Providence, the Divine Plan!"

The evident presence of self-affirmation, compassion, and thankful celebration in the gay community, even though frequently disguised, manifests not only the basic health there, but also the radical religious character latent in gay experience. But living creatively with homosexuality does not end with acceptance. It begins with it. And at least two further elements are essential for spiritual wholeness: association and action.

SOLIDARITY

Real and continuous contact with *both* gay and straight people is necessary for effective living in a world that is neither wholly straight nor gay. Isolation means loneliness and one or another form of estrangement, which is a way of saying incomplete development as a human person. The "healthy homosexual" man or woman can be shown to have a gay support group as well as heterosexual friends and acquaintances. The loner as well as the "heterophobe" is usually headed for problems.

Association finds expression in solidarity and friendship. Both are important, but it is friendship that is indispensable. Intimacy among friends is not restricted to genital experience; in fact, for many gays, "having sex" may be the least likely event in which they enjoy true closeness. Without true intimacy, the experience of physical, emotional, and spiritual closeness to someone, life is too easily reduced to the mechanical relationships we call games or simply deprived of all human warmth.

Developmentally, finding such lasting intimacy is especially important for the very young and the elderly — and especially difficult at times for gay men and women. The energy and natural gregariousness of youth offer opportunities for socializing that are often lacking to older women and men. Fortunately, groups such as SAGE (Senior Action in a Gay Environment, Inc.[12]) provide many valuable services and resources for senior gay men and lesbians, especially those who are homebound, confined to nursing homes, hospitals, or are otherwise isolated. These include home visits, educational programs, dinner-dances, newsletters, and personal correspondence. Similar organizations exist for teenagers in many cities. And while animal friends can never really substitute for human companionship, pets provide a source of true care and love for many older men and women, especially those who live outside larger urban centers whose lives would otherwise lack the blessing of closeness. (The therapeutic value of having pets is now widely recognized clinically. Similarly, the developmental value of pet-ownership is receiving more attention and should not be neglected as a spiritual as well as psychological resource.)

The computer age has added an electronic dimension to the possibilities of gay solidarity that can strengthen the personal and social bonds among lesbians and gay men separated by distance or circumstances — "networking" via personal computers. A variety of newspapers and newsletters reinforces the vital connections that support human interaction and friendship. Today, more than ever, there is no reason for anyone to remain isolated or lonely.

SERVICE

In all spirituality, as shall see later in greater detail, the natural outgrowth of solidarity and compassion is social action, usually expressed in some form of pursuit of justice. Not surprisingly, it is impossible for many gays and lesbians not to do something to improve the lot of their struggling brothers and sisters once they have experienced the real liberation of acceptance and radical affirmation in the midst of a supportive community. For some, the form action will take is political. For others, service of various kinds. Nowhere is this more true at present than in the volunteer support groups for persons with AIDS.

After twenty years, both gays and straights are still learning to work together for a better society rather than merely protesting injustices in order to reform a prejudicial legal system and to bring about new legislation guaranteeing equal rights and opportunity in housing, employment, and other areas of civil life. Similarly, serious and sincere dialogue with church leaders and theologians is slowly replacing merely polemical confrontations.

Gays also have to come to recognize that many of their difficulties and suffering result from the destructive agencies within gay culture itself. The struggle for liberation entails the correction of these elements, too — whether the defensive psychic and social structure erected by any beleaguered minority, or the deliberate exploitation of gays by other gays themselves. For gays, too, are the perpetuators as well as the victims of their own sexual myths and manipulative behavior. Here again, only the truth of lives well-lived can convince and liberate.

In religious language, the "vocation" of gays is thus not only to accept themselves as God accepts them, and to work to bring about an end to repression and injustice anywhere, but also to infuse the gay world itself with love and reconciliation.

REDEEMING THE GAY WORLD

Gay Christians need not forsake the gay world any more than any Christian need forsake the world in order to be saved. But like the Christian-in-general, the gay Christian, while in the world is not *of* it — that is, not its creature. Like other Christians, gay men and women must be *for* the world, including the gay world in so far as it is not wholly inimically to their own welfare or irreconcilably opposed to Christian values. The Christian is called (and sent) to any place where redemption is warranted.

The gay world is permeated with positive values, many of them, however, less evident than its defects and dangers — none of which I intend to minimize. But to overlook the generosity, compassion, community-feeling, and real love present there even in largely latent form would be an even greater disservice. Real human (and therefore Christian) values exist in the gay world, and it is thus redeemable and, to the extent that they are manifest and operative, in that measure redeemed and redemptive.

Again, like the large world of which it is a token, the gay world is a dangerous place, spiritually as well as morally and sometimes even physically. But as a microcosm, the gay world richly illustrates both the opportunity and means by which the Christian reconstruction of the world can proceed, especially in terms of the whole realm of sexuality.

Life in the so-called straight world can be bitter, or it can be the occasion for enjoyment and achievement for gay men and women not so much *as* gay, but primarily as persons who also happen to be gay. The cost of success, however, is perseverance, faithfulness, and integrity. The penalty for withdrawal, capitulation, and evasion will be not only a stunted social life, but the perpetuation of oppression from without and exploitation from within the gay community. On the other hand, a flippant militancy can also fan dwindling embers of prejudice into new flames of persecution. What is called for in the realm of action is judgment, skill, and authentic concern as well as courage and resilience.

For the most part, the "secret" of living with homosexuality — especially for those gays who are not blessed with outstanding talents, skills, or even courage — is a relatively simple thing: living with compassion and honesty, with oneself and others, both gay and straight. While no different in their need for love and justice, dignity and meaning, gays and lesbians often face obstacles no straight person is ever likely to encounter in the pursuit of happiness. Consequently, their ways of overcoming these obstacles will be to some extent distinctive. But straight people should have no great difficulty with that; the values and beliefs are common. Despite that fundamental sameness, for gays and lesbians the "courage to be" — the willingness to make life rich in meaning and devotion — also requires the strength to be different and the nerve to celebrate that difference as a gift and an opportunity.

NOTES

1. For references, see especially the works by Marmor, Bell and Weinberg, Masters and Johnson, and Karlen in the Resources for Further Reading, below, pp. 181ff.
2. Cf. the landmark study published by Drs. Alan Bell and Martin Weinberg with the apt and revealing title *Homosexualities: A Study of Diversity among Men and Women* (New York: Simon and Schuster, 1978).
3. Significantly, there is no corresponding word for "lesbian" to refer to male homosexuality. Despite some feeling to the contrary among women's groups, I don't think that *gay* should be given that function. Historically, it applied to both sexes and still does in common usage.

4. For a recent synopsis and critique of Dörner's views, see "Sexual Destinies," by Linda Murray, *Omni* (May, 1987): 100-28.
5. Catholic Social Welfare Commission, Catholic Bishops of England and Wales (Mt. Rainier, Md: New Ways Ministry, 1981), p. 12.
6. Ibid., p. 5.
7. Lionel Ovesey, *Homosexuality and Pseudohomosexuality*, New York: Science House, 1969. See also Lionel Ovesey and Sherwyn M. Woods, "Pseudohomosexuality and Homosexuality in Men: Psychodynamics as a Guide to Treatment," in Marmor, ed. cit., pp. 325-41.
8. A sympathetic portrayal of one such women can be found in Wallace Hamilton's romantic novel *Coming Out*, New York: Signet, 1977.
9. Martin and Lyon, op. cit., p. 29.
10. The words "homosexual," "heterosexual," and "bisexual" are, properly speaking, adjectives, not nouns, referring to one aspect of personality—sexual orientation. To use them as nouns reflects a common but wrong-headed propensity to equate personality with sexuality. Despite the existence of a homosexual subculture, a person is not "a" homosexual in anything like the sense of being "a" woman," "a" Republican or "an" Australian.
11. For further discussion, see below, pp. 60, 86-89.
12. For address, see Resources below, pp. 181ff. Also see below, pp. 92-94.

CHAPTER THREE

Living in a Straight World

WHAT we now call "Western Civilization" has been characterized for several thousand years by a virtual preoccupation with sex. As with law, politics, philosophy, medicine, science, education, and religion, in sexual matters the forebears of what we claim as our Judeo-Christian tradition were mainly the Greeks, the Jews, the Romano-Italic peoples, and the Germanic tribes of northwestern Europe. The Greeks and Romans contributed a certain enthusiasm for the varieties of sexual experience, while from the Jews and Germans we derived an often conflicting demand for control and restriction.

Our religious and ethical attitudes toward sexuality are particularly indebted to the severe, almost puritanical code of the patriarchal Jews which distinguished their worship and morality from those of surrounding peoples, especially, in the three pre-Christian centuries of Hellenic cultural influence and Alexandrian conquest, that of the Greeks.

While never totally successful, even in ancient times, within the last century this more or less monolithic sexual code has been eroded, if not cracked, by the pressure of the social sciences and psychiatry, coupled with the fracture of the supportive substrata of authoritarian philosophy and theology. But despite a shift in attitudes (the so-called "sexual revolution" of the 1960s and 70s), actual deviation, especially homosexuality, has by no means become tolerable to modern society as a whole. Gays and lesbians still live in an officially straight and therefore largely unsympathetic world. Although actual persecution may be unlikely, one of the many tragic effects of the growing AIDS epidemic has been a rekindling of harassment, forced disclosure, threats of internment, and a manifest escalation of attacks against so-called "gay rights" ordinances.

In this and the following chapter, I intend to explore a few possibilities with regard to sexual co-existence, presuming that the number of gay persons in our society will remain constant, as will the general disapproval of most other people. It may help to reduce mutual antagonism by examining some of the prevalent myths about homosexuality, those of both the straight and the gay world. But my central concern will be with how gays traverse the border between the gay and straight world without personal diminishment, a feat which will become more and more dependent upon a mutual willingness of gays and straights to co-exist, to evaluate attitudes and ideas, and, if necessary, to alter them.

A Legacy of Oppression

Homosexual behavior among men, and occasionally among women, has been strongly condemned in the civil and especially the religious laws of most western peoples throughout history.[1] Even in Greece, homosexual liaisons among adult males (in contrast to pedophilia) were generally considered to be a perversion. In Athens, Solon (639-559 B.C.) decreed the death penalty for the attempted seduction of youths. It is questionable, however, whether the sentence was ever carried out. Moreover, Greek attitudes were notoriously ambivalent. Mythology and Homeric tales are replete with tales of homosexual — as well as heterosexual — love, from Zeus and Ganymede (from whose name is derived the word "catamite") to Achilles and Patroclus. Upper-class Greek society was also more tolerant of adult homosexuality than were the lower classes.[2]

Among the ancient Jews, the Torah prescribed death as the punishment for homosexual acts (Lev. 20:13) — probably by stoning. Again, however, there are no accounts of actual executions in the Bible, unlike instances of heterosexual punishment for crimes such as adultery and rape. (The divine destruction of Sodom and Gomorrah was probably not merely because of "sodomy," even if such a thing were actually attempted by the otherwise vicious Sodomites.[3])

The New Testament also records no actual punishments for homosexual behavior, nor do any early Christian documents, despite several general condemnations. The first mention of the death penalty within the Christian era occurs in an imperial decree from the year 342 A.D. An edict of Theodosius in 390 specified burning at the stake for both homosexual offenses and heresy. Officially, burning would remain the ordinary legal penalty for over a thousand years to come, but few if any actual instances of execution can be cited before the fifteenth century.

It was not until the time of the Spanish Inquisition that homosexual acts were punished to any large extent by death, but even then leniency was the general rule in practice. Perhaps fifty to one hundred persons were executed in all. During the era of the Reformation and the wars of religion and up to the nineteenth century, possibly two hundred more victims went to the stake or gallows, or were beheaded, drowned, strangled, or even buried alive.

Compared to the *millions* of Muslims, Jews, Greek Orthodox Christians, Albigensians, Protestants, Catholics, "witches," and even real criminals judicially murdered between the tenth and twentieth centuries, comparatively few homosexual men and women were killed. But actual executions should not be taken as the sole index of oppression; confiscation, imprisonment, exile, torture, mutilation, fines, and public humiliation were likewise employed — when, as with capital punishment, it so suited the state or church. Perhaps the most destructive form of oppression was (and is) the constant weight of civil and ecclesiastical reprobation loaded on homosexual persons, whether publicly or in the solitude of their own minds.

The single most horrible instance of gay persecution occurred, not surprisingly, during Hitler's Third Reich.

Known homosexual persons in Germany and occupied countries were rounded up and sent to concentration camps. Forced to wear pink triangles to proclaim their crime — similar to the Jews' yellow Star of David — over 220,000 gays were slaughtered by the Nazis, according to reliable sources. Even when "liberated" by the Allies, those who survived the holocaust, being considered criminals, were not allowed to receive compensation.[4]

Today, as in past ages, cruel and unusual punishment is still meted out to gays, often in the form of lengthy prison sentences. But official acts of condemnation do not comprise the major harassment, oppression, and daily stress that gays must endure or succumb to. Although no longer executed (save in officially Muslim nations), they are often abused by police, the press, and politicians. Homosexual "witch hunts," instigated even in recent decades to ruin or threaten political figures or to bolster the image of their rivals, have generally destroyed only the little fry who lacked sufficient power, money, or prestige to avoid being netted. More subtly, known homosexual persons are often denied equal protection under law.

The selective enforcement of laws equally applicable to heterosexual and homosexual "crimes" often singles out gays for punishment and public disgrace. The armed forces "separate" admitted gays from service with a "less than honorable" discharge, if not dishonorably after a court martial. Employees of all kinds, but especially teachers and government officials have been summarily fired even on the mere suspicion of being homosexual. Others are forced to resign. Many seminaries (both Christian and Jewish) and religious orders still refuse to accept candidates who are or who appear to be homosexual; suspected homosexuality is likewise sufficient warrant for expulsion (a major plot element in the gripping play and movie *Mass Appeal*).[5] Gay rabbis, priests, and ministers are likely to be deprived of their calls. For some victims of such thorough social oppression, society's final act of vengeance is the coroner's verdict of suicide, and not infrequently of murder.

The death of Robert Hillsborough in San Francisco in June,

1977, tragically illustrated how anti-gay sentiment expressed in a publicly irresponsible manner can contribute to violence and crime. In the midst of the anti-gay rights campaign centered on a Dade County, Florida, referendum, Hillsborough was singled out for an unprovoked, brutal, and unjust attack by four youths. His killers stabbed Hillsborough fifteen times with a hunting knife.

Two of the assailants were convicted, one of second-degree murder, the other of aggravated assault. Another was granted immunity for testifying against his companions, while the fourth was tried in juvenile court. In connection with the murder, a five-million-dollar lawsuit was filed against Anita Bryant and her Save Our Children crusade by Hillsborough's mother and his lover. While unsuccessful, the suit points out how pressure against gays generated by self-righteous citizens all-too publicly concerned about law and order can become, ironically, an incentive to crime.[6] For it easily justifies violent abuse of those already targeted for hostility and persecution. Even sadder is the fact that such has been the perennial lot of minority groups throughout the long history of "civilization."[7]

Similarly, the 1979 verdict of "voluntary manslaughter" and the relative leniency of the seven year and eight months prison sentence given Dan White for the deliberate shooting of San Francisco Mayor George Moscone and Harvey Milk infuriated the gay community and many straight people. Milk was a well-known gay rights activist elected to the San Francisco Board of Supervisors. White, a former fireman and policeman, had also been elected to the Board of Supervisors, but resigned because, he said, the salary was insufficient to support his family.

Moscone accepted his resignation, but four days later White asked to be reinstated. Milk persuaded Moscone not to reappoint White, who had been a major obstacle to many of Moscone's programs. The following day, White went to City Hall, where he shot and killed Moscone in his office, then methodically invited Milk to his own office, where he also shot and killed the gay Supervisor.

The defense pleaded "diminished capacity," and apparently

convinced that White's excessive "junk-food" diet had contributed to temporary insanity, the jury returned the verdict of voluntary manslaughter. Two riots broke out in San Francisco when the verdict was announced. An angry crowd of gays stormed City Hall, where they were turned back by police. Later that night, squads of riot police countered by invading Castro Street, the predominantly gay district of San Francisco, where they randomly attacked pedestrians and patrons of gay bars with night sticks. A hundred gay men and sixty-one policemen had to be hospitalized.

White himself served five years of his sentence and was released on parole in 1984. The same year, a film commemorating the slain gay activist, *The Times of Harvey Milk*, won an Academy Award for the best documentary film feature. White returned to San Francisco a year later. But in October of 1986, unable to find work and despondent, he committed suicide.

Gay Resistance and Liberation

It is worth noting that the riot and desperate resistance to police assault by San Francisco's gays in 1979 occurred exactly a decade after the "Stonewall Riot" that followed a harassment raid on a New York gay bar in 1969. Unexpectedly, the customers resisted arrest, and with the days of minor rioting that ensued, the "gay rights" movement in America began in earnest. Soon, gays everywhere were offering increased resistance to both overt and clandestine oppression, often aided by civil liberties groups. In the decade that followed, legal action against the military, city, state, and federal governments, industries, social organizations, and even religious bodies effected dramatic changes, as did protests, demonstrations, petitions, and campaigns. The emergence of a visible "gay press" added to the growing power of resistance. In 1973, the National Gay Task Force was founded. It is still the largest gay civil rights organization in the country, although many more have appeared since.

By 1979, despite the vituperations of Anita Bryant's anti-gay propaganda and the counter-offensive of conservative Americans led by fundamentalist preachers, the achievement of civil rights as well as the political influence of gays and lesbians had reached an all-time high. Often the specific aims of such efforts were not well-defined; sometimes they were acutely focused. And although nothing like a unified gay political coalition emerged from these efforts, overall the movement for acceptance seems to have brought about a mood of increased tolerance of homosexuality as a part of life in America, at least in major urban areas.

Celebrations such as Gay Pride week, the annual commemoration of the Stonewall Riot, with its speeches, workshops, parties, and parade, have accomplished much in the way of softening public attitudes. Even in the wake of the AIDS scare of the mid-'eighties, and despite evident setbacks in public acceptability, "Gay Day" parades concluding Gay Pride Week at the end of June still bring out hundreds of thousands of gays, lesbians, and sympathetic straight people in most major American cities.

Nevertheless, the nationwide swing toward more conservative politics in the 'eighties, along with the near-panic over AIDS, seriously blunted the edge of gay liberation efforts in the United States and elsewhere. The public and political effort to end discrimination and oppression is not likely to disappear, however. For, in addition to its necessary role in achieving greater toleration, such active involvement also increases solidarity with other oppressed minorities and represents a healthy form of participation in democratic social process. By direct action and support, gays continue to appropriate their own political destiny — a requirement for responsible citizenship in a free society. In the wake of the AIDS tragedy, such efforts are even more needed to ensure vital services and to bolster individual and collective self-esteem.

As gay women and men assume a more visible place in society, able leadership in the gay community will become even more important. Those who now merely, if artfully, verbalize gays' complaints against the straight world are not likely to be as able to sponsor positive contributions to a saner, more humane world embracing both gays and straights. Further, it will take immense discernment and skill to guide constructive collaboration with the straight world without sacrificing the valuable counter-cultural elements in the gay world — elements laden with corrective, prophetic potential.

CULTURAL OPPRESSION AND EMANCIPATION

Political oppression and resistance are not the only dialectical factors involved in the struggle toward true sexual emancipation. Cultural oppression of gays has been no less prevalent, and possibly more damaging to their human dignity; cultural resistance has been no less needed.

Gays have been ridiculed and lampooned since the comedies of Aristophanes and the stories of Lucan and Horace, more often than not, viciously. Until comparatively recent times, despite occasional attempts at sympathetic, even honest treatment, novels, plays, and films have generally portrayed gays in stereotypical poses. Gay men were more often than not effeminate "fags," fey and not only unhappy, but dead by the last chapter, act, or final reel. The same was true of lesbians, who tended to appear "butch" and callous as well as not a little sick. Few homosexual roles in film or on stage even attempted to present a truly human, healthy, or remotely well-adjusted gay person — despite the fact that many well-known screen and stage writers have been homosexual.

The paying public got what it wanted. As a mirror of their situation, films, plays, and most novels have reflected a distorted image of gays' lives, merely reinforcing popular myths and perpetuating stereotypes. Gay films, magazines, and novels, mainly a species of soft to hard-core pornography, have often been similarly oppressive and distorted, in so far as they featured counter-myths and stereotypes, fantasies, and sexual escapism. While possibly more understandable, the market-determined themes and treatment in gay literature and films are no more excusable than those dredged up by the straight establishment. Both are detrimental to the formation of healthy attitudes, values, and patterns of behavior among gay women and men, pandering to the lowest levels of prurience and escapism, rather than offering plausible models for authentic admiration and imitation.

Instead of burying themselves in the vast sands of the television wasteland in search of alternative entertainment, however, many gay men and women have chosen to participate fully in the best cultural life accessible in society, exercising critical judgment and expressing their view about the presentation of gay as well as other themes. For instance, the gay Media-watch, established to detect prejudicial treatment (mainly on television), far from being a form of censorship, was itself a responsible exercise of freedom of expression. The Gay Task Force of the American Library Association has worked for many years to assure the presence on library shelves across the nation of high-quality material dealing with homosexuality. Individuals, too, have not only demanded fair representation in the media, but have shown their appreciation for honest attempts to explore the gay situation.

In this country and elsewhere, artists involved in the media and theater have also struggled to correct the distorted image of gays not only in major films, but perhaps especially in gay-produced entertainment. Combatting both the insipid and often pornographic image of gay life typical of films and plays a generation ago, gay and conscientious straight directors and writers have increasingly succeeded in depicting realistic characters caught up in believable situations, whether serious or light-hearted. The past two decades provided many outstanding examples, among them *The L-Shaped Room, A Taste of Honey, Sunday Bloody Sunday, The Naked Civil Servant,* and *Maurice* from England; the Canadian feature *Outrageous;* and the superb U.S. documentaries *Word Is Out* and *The Times of Harvey Milk.* Low-budget classics such as the vintage *Saturday Night at the Baths* and more recently English import, *My Beautiful Laundrette* and

Waiting for the Moon, sometimes enjoy unexpected popular acclaim. After the commercial success of the film adaptations of Mart Crowley's play *The Boys in the Band* and John Herbert's *Fortune and Men's Eyes, Making Love, Personal Best,* and *Partners* followed as Hollywood's more or less honest attempt to portray gay and lesbian love in a positive manner. More recently, the brilliant *Kiss of the Spider Woman* gained international recognition and many awards. Even films made for television have explored dimensions of the gay world, such as *Consenting Adult* and the excellent Canadian production *The Truth about Alex.*

As gay themes in cinema matured (as did the audiences), the theater world moved ahead rapidly with *A Chorus Line, The Fifth of July, Streamers, Bent,* and *Torch Song Trilogy* among other plays. (The then-shocking musical classic *Hair!* had, of course, already dealt with a lead character's homosexuality in a compassionately humorous vein back in 1967.) In the late 80's, a new genre of gay-focused drama appeared in response to the AIDS crisis, much of it excellent theater as well as a much needed educational opportunity for both gay and straight audiences, significantly in this regard *As Is, The Normal Heart,* and *The AIDS Show,* which was broadcast over national public television.

TACIT OPPRESSION

Oppression need not be overt, nor even consciously in the mind of victim or oppressor to be effective; jokes and pointed remarks have always been used to put down despised groups of all kinds: "Can anything good come out of Nazareth?" The most insidious and destructive examples of society's negation of gays are probably covert forms of indoctrination. The emergence of the feminist liberation movement has illuminated this shadowy side of social conditioning with regard to childhood experiences, which are even more problematic for gays and lesbians than for straight women.

Children's play is not merely fun and games; in every culture, childhood is also a rehearsal period for acquiring skills and learning roles for later social existence. Typically (or, more accurately, stereotypically), little girls are given "baby" dolls that now urinate and vomit and are encouraged to play house. They are presented with tea-sets and tiny ovens, frilly aprons and cardboard or plastic "people" dolls with extensive wardrobes. They are discouraged from roughhousing, climbing trees, playing with toy weapons, or engaging in other unladylike occupations. Boys, of course, are encouraged to do everything girls are not supposed to. They are given footballs, toy tools, cars, trucks, trains, and fire engines, as well as a variety of guns, planes, tanks, and other war toys but are not allowed to play with dolls past a very tender age, nor do any of the "silly" things girls do, such as learning how to cook, sew, shop, clean house, or tend babies.

While it would be absurd, and in fact impossible, to change drastically the child-rearing practices of our culture, it should be realized that the attitudes conveyed by such conditioning embody highly questionable assumptions about masculine and feminine roles, behavior, and status in society, many of which *should* be changed. Many child psychologists as well as feminist and humanist leaders campaign tirelessly for such changes.

Certain attitudes are particularly inimical to full human development and need radical adjustment, for instance, the myth that men (and, ergo, little boys) are tough and probably dirty, logical, unemotional, competitive, and better than women (and, ergo, little girls), and must therefore dominate them. Women are, by contrast, weak, soft, emotionally fragile, needful of protection, guidance, and a strong male presence to serve and obey.

Truly changed attitudes (i.e., real conversion) tend to endure. Conversely, trends, fads, and fashions are seasonal enthusiasms soon discarded, often for their opposites. Thus, despite a brief flare-up of media attention, by the end of the decade the "new image" of the early "80s male" — sensitive, gentle, cultured, respectful of women's rights, etc., had fallen victim to other androgynous themes and the resurgent *machismo* of *Rambo* and his ilk. Similarly, entrenched nineteenth-century fantasies like the myth of the nuclear family and stereotypical gender roles have survived for some time and will continue powerfully underpinning much of the oppressive sexual conditioning in Western society despite the fact that they are neither Christian nor even healthy. Translated into adult behavior, they emerge as operational beliefs such as that of male supremacy — the notion that women exist to satisfy the male's sexual needs which, being irrepressible if not insatiable, must inevitably find genital expression given even the slightest opportunity.

To all appearances, a good deal of male adolescent energy is still devoted to creating such opportunities, or, in the case of young women, passively accepting or even avoiding them. And, no doubt, the actual situation is still more likely one of a mutual fear of inadequacy coupled with a sense of pressure to perform, often upheld by noisy bravado and accounts of previous exploits. Converted into behavioral values, such a combination of factors has ruined countless marriages and created crucifying feelings of inferiority among both gay and straight men and women.

"Pseudohomosexuality" is, in many cases, a way out of the sexual rat-race for straight men who cannot or will not conform to the expectations of the *macho* stereotype. The "feminine" values of true homosexual males, especially those who are not effeminate, challenge the male mystique even more severely. The usual response is violent repudiation, whether verbal or physical.

Lesbians are even more threatening to images of male superiority for, in effect, the message they embody is that men are sexually superfluous, if not an annoyance. The *macho* rejoinder has been to elevate photographic lesbianism to the level of sexual fantasy in "men's" magazines, reinforcing the myth that all women are merely sexual toys. But the dominant male image also forbids admitting, much less expressing, any deep affection for other men as well as women, if for no other reason than the deep fear of being thought "queer."

One of the signal contributions the mere presence of gay men and women offer to a society dominated by demonic sexual images and ideologies is the concrete critique of such myths and stereotypes. In this respect, homosexuality is a counter-cultural corrective, and to that extent, prophetic.

GAY MYTHS AND STEREOTYPES

The distorted thinking, projections, and unreal images that plague the whole realm of sexuality trouble male-female relationships seriously; they also create particularly difficult situation for gays. By *myths*, I am here referring to fanciful and prejudicial misconceptions about gays' sexual identity, roles, and behavior, which are shared by a large segment of the population, including some gays themselves. Similarly, *stereotypes* are images uncritically thought to be representative of all gay persons and hence of each. Myths, based on stereotypical thinking, determine various attitudes and behavior, most of which are unfortunate in their consequences, and not for gays alone.

The most obvious and pervasive stereotypes identify gays in terms of inverted gender roles: male gays are thought to be effeminate, arch, and willowy "fairies" and "faggots," while lesbians are rough, mannish, close-cropped "dykes." Various corollaries follow; the (erroneous) belief that gays can be recognized by clothing, body type, a certain "veiled" look in their eyes, the way they strike matches or examine their fingernails. The stereotypical "fruit" is a hairdresser, interior decorator, ballet dancer, or actor — the "les" or "lesbo" is a truck-driver, wrestler, or telephone installer. Sexual behavior is imagined to follow lines of inverted heterosexual roles (themselves largely mythical): an active, aggressive "male" and a passive, receptive "female." A further corollary is the belief that gays are sex-obsessed, their whole existence centered on bedding down as quickly and as often as they can with someone. Or anyone.

Most myths and stereotypes have a core of fact; the truth here is that some, if very few, gays *are* effeminate, mannish, sex-obsessed or what-have-you. But the far larger fact is that the great majority of gay men and lesbians are just like everyone else, except for their sexual preferences, and in that different not so much in kind as in degree. When thinking of a "typical" gay person, then, we might as well include Wyatt Earp and Emily Dickinson alongside Oscar Wilde and Gertrude Stein.

Even so, it nevertheless seems to be the case that gay men as a whole are in fact less aggressive and have greater sensitivity than equally representative straights. On matched personality tests, gays frequently (not always) score lower on aggression — Billy the Kid notwithstanding — and higher on aesthetic awareness, the appreciation of beauty. Hence, it would seem that many gays may "naturally" gravitate to the arts. But many also gravitate to the ministry and military.

Less is known about lesbians than gay men (perhaps because most sex researchers have been male). But at least with regard to male homosexuality, a man comfortable with his sexual orientation, however large or small an element in his self-awareness, is likely to be more open than the *macho* male (and no doubt his female equivalent) to realms of human experience foreclosed to the latter by the necessity of preserving the image of "he-man" (or "she-woman") toughness — an image lampooned as much by the "rhinestone cowboy" stars of country music fame as it is by the motorcycle club members who favor "leather and chains" gay bars.

Among other societal myths concerning homosexuality (sometimes shared by gays) are the beliefs that homosexual orientation is somehow chosen; that it is (conversely) a disease that "spreads," can be caught by the unwary or unprotected, and increases with toleration; that it is a permanent, static condition; that it is "only a phase"; that it is caused by something or someone; that gays are inevitably promiscuous and that, as a result, gay relationships are unstable and short-lived; and, most destructive of all, that gays are immoral child-molesters and perverts who imperil the existence of the family and the common good. Even a cursory examination can reveal the hollowness of such notions, many of which seem to be founded on fear and ignorance and continue to exist for no other reason than to bolster prejudice and discriminatory attitudes.

CHOICE VERSUS DISCOVERY

Earlier, I devoted considerable discussion to the elements of human sexuality. It should be clear by now that *neither* homosexual nor heterosexual orientation is deliberately chosen, but both are acquired determinations over which the individual exercises little initial conscious direction. Homosexuality can be chosen only in the sense that men or women, recognizing their orientation, either accept it and validate it or reject and suppress it. Since, further, homosexuality is not contagious, nor can people be "converted" from heterosexuality to homosexuality past the end of the adolescent period of sexual development, a person's sexual orientation is not basically subject to major alteration, whether voluntary or involuntary. In the words of the pastoral statement of the Catholic Bishops of England and Wales, "In the case of true homosexuals or 'inverts', professional therapy may be helpful to assist them in accepting their condition positively, but therapy should never be suggested in a way that raises false expectations of a reverse or modification of the homosexual condition."[8]

Despite well-known claims of success, lasting sexual reorientation thus seems to be highly questionable in principle as well as in fact, whether attempted by means of behavioral modification, hypnosis, psychoanalysis, or other forms of therapy, one of the more recent being called in all seriousness "Aesthetic Realism." The exception appears to be cases of pseudohomosexuality, a form of homosexual fascination experienced primarily if not exclusively by heterosexual males, probably as compensation for feared sexual inadequacy or other deficiencies, as mentioned earlier. Re-orienting a truly homosexual person is not only another matter, it is almost certainly doomed to failure, *even* among highly motivated clients. Independent follow-up studies have shown that initial "successes" generally revert back to their fundamental orientation after a period of time.[9]

How many gays and lesbians would want to change even if they could by simply "pushing a button" is not at all certain. What is certain, at least from my own interviews as well as other published accounts, is that very many would not.

Regarding the so-called danger of increasing the incidence of homosexuality by tolerating gays and lesbians, anthropological research indicates that, despite wide differences in cultural attitudes, neither toleration nor suppression determines the basic incidence of homosexuality or homosexual behavior, only their public manifestation. In fact, some of the most tolerant societies have shown the least incidence of both.

PROMISCUITY

Another commonplace myth is that gays, especially men, are notoriously promiscuous. It is probably true that most homosexual liaisons among men, especially the young, are unstable, like those of their heterosexual counterparts. That is, they are *intended* to be brief, noncommittal affairs of mutual and self-indulgent enjoyment. But many, possibly most gay men and women also hope for a lasting relationship with one other person. And many in fact achieve their goal — far more than once believed by researchers (whose main avenue of information often lay through bars and baths). This is especially true of lesbians. But as gay men mature, they, too, tend to form more permanent relationships and "settle down."

Being personally acquainted with a number of gay and lesbian couples, some of whom have lived together for twenty years or more, I find the charge of instability to be one of the most unfortunate and unjust myths. The typical theological attitude in this regard is especially lamentable. For instance, a leading moralist recently wrote that permanent bonds rooted in deep interpersonal love between homosexual males are rare, but he conceded that in terms of an alternate lifestyle of promiscuity, such unions can be tolerated as "a lesser evil." The irony consists in the fact that such unions have been roundly denounced by conventional moralists as the *greater* evil. Further, one of the reasons churchmen believe lasting gay unions to be rare is that those admitting to them have often been accused of living in sin, denied the sacraments as impenitent sinners, and sometimes literally driven out of the church. In terms of forcing permanent relationships underground, as well as inadvertently increasing promiscuity among gays, the church is not guiltless.

Casual and indiscriminate sexual encounters and lifelong "monogamous" relationships actually represent extremes of a whole spectrum of gay relationships. Many close relationships are not genitally expressed at all. Others which find or are built upon sexual expression are relatively long-term affairs — from a few weeks or a month or two to a matter of years. But such relationships are not promiscuous in the customary sense of that world. From one perspective, the "unions" are facsimiles of a great many straight liaisons — minus the social and ecclesiastical rituals of serial bonding and splitting. From that viewpoint, these relationships are indeed "another kind of love" — affectionate, caring, and responsible, neither promiscuous nor an ape of heterosexual marriage.

Differing from the classical pattern of heterosexual unions, gay liaisons have proved difficult to categorize in terms of ordinary Western social institutions.[10] Consequently moralists in particular are at a disadvantage in evaluating them. Surely one of the major tasks of the gay Christian community will be to explore such distinctive elements of gay experience, raising them to the level of critical consciousness in the light of the Gospel of Christ as well as the demands and unique situation of the gay world.

FAMILY VALUES

Finally, if not completely, it is a prevalent belief that homosexuality, or, more concretely, *gays* are dangerous, especially to children, and to social values in general, especially those of the family. In fact, the vast majority of gay men and women are ethically conscientious, law-abiding, and otherwise valuable members of society. Some criminals are homosexual — apparently Clyde Barrow, Babyface Nelson, and John Dillinger were; most apparently are not. Sex-offenses involving true molestation of adults and children are committed by less than one percent of the homosexual population — a figure roughly equivalent to that of the offenders in the heterosexual population, which is ten times larger. This simply means that nine out of ten sex-offenders, including child-molesters, are straight. (The sexual "crimes" gays — usually men — are accused of almost invariably involve the private activities of consenting adults, acts now "decriminalized" in many states and nearly every civilized nation on earth. Lesser offenses typically include solicitation, loitering, and "disorderly conduct" — such as, for example, dancing in a gay bar.)

Regarding the family itself, some gays have experienced rejection and hostility from parents and relatives; others, tragically, have broken off all contact with their families, either out of fear of rejection or in order to spare their parents grief and suffering. But many gays retain excellent family relations, whether or not their homosexuality or their life-style is approved of. Many more would like to.

Often, gay men and women devote years of their lives to the care of aged or infirm parents. Gay men and women are also increasingly petitioning to adopt children on the grounds that a child's having a homosexual parent (or parents) is preferable to having none. (There is no evidence that sexual orientation can be influenced simply by having a homosexual parent; presumably, most gays had straight parents. I know of several instances in which children reared by gay or lesbian parents have developed into happily heterosexual adults.) Among other advantages natural or adopted children will probably receive from gay parents is freedom from the scourge of homophobia.

Thus, despite much sanctimonious scare-talk about increased acceptance of homosexuality weakening family ties, it is even more likely that a saner attitude in this respect will actually strengthen the family. It also remains true, however, that unaccepting attitudes towards a child's homosexuality on the part of one or both parents can seriously disrupt a family. In such cases, parental fear, ignorance, intolerance, and shame typically play a major role. Even here, however, time tends to bring about a healing of familial wounds, as Ann Muller has shown in her excellent study *Parents Matter*.[11] (Significantly, in our still patriarchal society, both the mothers and fathers of gay male children show much greater acceptance over time than do the parents of lesbians.)

The pioneering work of Betty Fairchild and other advocates of parental acceptance has done much to educate and assist families caught up in the not-uncommon turmoil of an adolescent's discovery of her or his homosexuality. Local chapters of organizations such as the National Federation of Parents and Friends of Gays, and the Federation of Parents and Friends of Lesbians and Gays also provide resource materials, speakers, counseling, and "rap groups" to aid both parents and children attempting to cope with "coming out."[12]

SEEING GAY

The primary means of destroying myths about gays and gay life resides in *looking*. For gays, looking into themselves honestly, with willingness to affirm the special qualities, talents, skills, and interests that make each person unique, but also willing to acknowledge their deficiencies and defects and to begin correcting them where possible. Honest discernment also requires looking carefully at the standardized life-styles which the gay ghetto offers, then deciding whether to fit into the stereotypes or risk becoming an "oddball" by creating one's own destiny.

For straight people, it means looking honestly at their own prejudices, personal fears, and negative attitudes as sources of actual or potential oppression. Even in the face of the obvious role-playing so pervasive in gay culture, straight persons should recall that each human being is a distinct individual with a unique personality, talents, capacities, and problems. The masks and ruses straights encounter in the ghetto are often assumed because *they* and their kind have long since been the aggressor.

In the final analysis, the real problem of homosexuality is primarily one of *straight* liberation — liberation from the myths, the stereotypical thinking, and the consequent forms of discrimination that, in turn, engender defensive postures among gays. Disabusing people of prejudicial notions can only be achieved, as I noted before, by education, which thus becomes a tactical necessity in any strategy for gay emancipation. Self-education is, of course, a vital precondition and a task especially important for teachers, counselors, and clergy. (Select references are listed in the Resources for Further Reading below, pp. 181ff.)

Gays can (and must) also do much by the witness of their lives and behavior to demonstrate the falsity of the myths and prejudices that demean them. Rather than coming out of the ghetto defensively, this means coming out proudly and honestly, willing to work and, if need be, to suffer in order to achieve a more liberated society and ultimately a saner world.

NOTES

1. Notable exceptions have existed, even in the Church, as Dr. John Boswell's research has disclosed (see *Christianity, Social Tolerance, and Homosexuality,* Chicago: University of Chicago Press, 1980, passim). Cf. also the more recent and extraordinary study by B. R. Burg, *Sodomy and the Pirate Tradition: English Sea Rovers in the Seventeenth-Century Caribbean* (New York and London: New York University Press, 1984), in which he shows that homosexuality and homosexual behavior were shown extensive tolerance both in England and in the West Indies from the Jacobean accession to the nineteenth century.

2. The classic study of this area is K. J. Dover, *Greek Homosexuality,* Cambridge: Harvard University Press, 1978. Cf. also Arno Karlen, "Homosexuality in History," in Marmor, ed. cit., pp. 78-80.

3. See below, pp. 101-2.

4. Cf. Louis Crompton, "Gay Genocide: From Leviticus to Hitler," Module #10, Salvatorian Justice and Peace Commission, Milwaukee: no date, p. 8. Cf. also Arno Karlen, op. cit., pp. 313-15, 334.

5. For a survey of recent attitudes among Catholic religious communities, see *Who's Entering Religious Life?* Chicago: National Conference of Religious Vocation Directors (1307 S. Wabash Ave., Suite 350, Chicago, IL 60605), 1987.

6. The much publicized role played by singer Anita Bryant in instigating the anti-gay "crusades" of the mid-70s became the background of Patricia Nell Warren's strangely prophetic novel *The Beauty Queen* (New York: William Morrow, 1978). After the breakup of her marriage a few years later, Bryant expressed regret over her previous actions in a dramatic about-face.

7. For similar accounts, see David Kopay and Perry Young, op. cit., pp. 219-20, and John McNeill, *The Church and the Homosexual*, Kansas City: Sheed, Andrews and McMeil, Inc., 1979, p. 158.

8. Op. cit., p. 12.

9. Cf. Judd Marmor, M.D., "Homosexuality and Sexual Orientation Disturbances," in *The Sexual Experience*, Benjamin J. Sadock, Harold I. Kaplan and Alfred M. Freedman, eds., Baltimore: The Williams and Wilkins Co., 1976, pp. 374-91. See also the discussion in the works by Karlen, Churchill, Ovesey, Weinberg, Freedman, and Hoffman listed in the Resources for Further Reading below, pp. 181ff.

10. Nonetheless, for a pioneering and detailed scientific evaluation of the varieties and quality of homosexual relationships, see the important volume by Bell and Weinberg, *Homosexualities: A Study of Diversity among Men and Women*, op. cit. Burg's study of homosexuality among English pirates and buccaneers, *Sodomy and the Pirate Tradition*, op. cit., is also instructive.

11. Ann Muller, *Parents Matter: Parents' Relationships with Lesbian Daughters and Gay Sons*, Tallahassee: Naiad Press, 1987.

12. For addresses, see Resources for Further Reading below, pp. 181ff. See especially Betty Fairchild and Nancy Hayward, *Now that You Know: What Every Parent Should Know about Homosexuality*, New York: Harcourt Brace Jovanovich, 1979, and Dr. Charles Silverstein, *A Family Matter: A Parents' Guide to Homosexuality*, New York: McGraw-Hill, 1977.

CHAPTER FOUR

Living in a Gay World

LIKE members of any persecuted minority, many gay men and women have long since gathered together into supportive and protective groups for social purposes and sometimes simply to live in proximity. The creation of what many gays themselves call the "gay ghetto" is thus at least partially a consequence of society's hostility towards gays. And, as is true of any ghetto, the gay ghetto manifests the characteristic qualities of those who populate it — including both the most and least admirable traits.

Increasingly greater attention is being paid to the dual social context of homosexuality by psychologists and sociologists. (By "dual" I mean both the general heterosexual environment and the specifically homosexual milieu.) Theologians have been much slower to assess homosexual behavior in terms of social structures and dynamics. Consequently, most religious literature still focuses on individual acts, more often than not taken abstractly—the so-called "objective morality."[1] But society provides the foundation as well as the context for all moral decisions and acts. Understanding the spiritual and moral dimensions of the homosexual world thus requires a look at the gay ghetto as well as the influence on it of straight society.

MICROCOSM AND MACROCOSM

Ordinarily, the world of lesbians and gay men is the same world everyone else shares; they read the same newspapers, shop at the same supermarkets, watch the same television shows, and attend the same churches as their heterosexual neighbors. But as a subculture, the gay world has its own language, customs, beliefs, values, and institutions, in many — perhaps most — instances fairly sharply divided along male-female lines. An element of conflict with many customs, values, beliefs, and institutions of the dominant straight society also gives the gay world the character of a counterculture. Language, however, presents the clearest instance of the distinctiveness of gay society and also provides a useful index to important ideas, cultural patterns, and values.

Throughout the preceding chapters I have used words such as "gay" and "straight," "homosexual" and "heterosexual," which, whether slang or technical, are generally well known. But for those readers unfamiliar with the language of the gay world, some explanation of less common terms will be helpful enough to justify a brief digression.

Gay is slang or "street talk" for *homosexual,* and often implies *male.* It, too, is an adjective, but is used frequently as a noun. Obscure but ancient in origin, *gay* was often used of women as well as men of various sexual "persuasions" and occupations, usually suggesting a certain looseness of morals. Today, no specific moral judgment is implied, but in the gay world, the associations are favorable and the word is greatly preferred to technical terms such as "homosexual," "invert," etc. *Gay* often refers to life-style or to the whole homosexual subculture. It further designates persons who have accepted their homosexuality as an integral part of their personalities, and are privately and to a greater or lesser extent publicly comfortable being known as homosexual. In distinction from persons whose homosexuality is hidden, repressed, or clandestine, gays are said to be "out of the closet" or simply "out." Often, being publicly "out" is expressed by direct political activity, but not all gays are militants or political activists.

Lesbian is a term most homosexual women prefer in describing themselves. It was adopted in memory of the Greek poet Sappho of Lesbos, an island in the Aegean Sea. Sappho lived in the seventh century B.C., the first recorded woman poet, and the first romantic poet. She herself was married and had a daughter. Over the years, she gathered around herself a poetic circle of young women who worshipped Aphrodite and the Muses. Sappho eulogized many of her students in amorous, rhapsodic verse, only a few hundred lines of which have survived. She may or may not have been homosexual.

Straight is common jargon for heterosexual, both male and female, with the usual implication of exclusivity — a gross oversimplification. The "straight world" thus means everything not manifestly gay. *Straight* can also be used as a noun or an adjective. (Occasionally, gays refer disparagingly to straight men and women as "breeders," an ironic jab at those who deride gay relationships as sterile.)

Coming out refers to the recognition, acceptance, and acknowledgment of homosexual preference, usually in terms of an actual event. Being "brought out" means being sexually initiated into the gay world, usually by a more experienced partner; it does not refer to passing, single, or childhood experiences. "Being out" refers to the state of identification as gay, usually in some kind of public context. What gays are out *of* is "the closet," that is, the condition of secrecy. "Closet queen" is most often a term of mild contempt — less mild if a reference to a homosexual male who actively pretends to be heterosexual in order to avoid discrimination. (*Queen* or *quean* originally meant a female prostitute, but was later applied to homosexual men; today it especially refers to men who affect a regal and effeminate attitude.)   *Lover* usually means a more or less permanent, faithful sexual partner, as opposed to a "trick," "number," or "john" someone might encounter during a "one-night stand." (In general, these terms apply appropriately to males only.) *Tricking* means picking up a casual sex partner on a non-payment basis.

Trade refers to a male, frequently claiming to be heterosexual, who seeks sex with a gay partner but who refuses to perform any acts he construes to be "feminine." A *hustler* is a male prostitute who provides sexual services for men (as well as women) for money, but who may not be homosexual himself. Many hustlers are also trade, that is, they will perform only what they consider to be the "male" role in sexual relations. Some hustlers are vicious thugs who prey on homosexual clients, beating and robbing them, sometimes resorting to blackmail and even to murder. A *john* is the paying partner of either a male or female prostitute. Someone in "retail" is usually an exclusively gay hustler.

Cruising once simply meant actively searching for a sex partner by male or female prostitutes or just "amateurs" interested in a brief, non-committal encounter. In gay circles, cruising now mainly refers to the visual scrutiny of a potential partner, sometimes including mutually provocative eye-contact, whether at a bar, the theater or opera, in a bookstore, cafe, public lavatory ("tea-room"), or just about anywhere else.

Camp means an ironic style of commentary or deportment, whether expressed in gestures, speech, dress, or even decor. Once a theatrical term for exaggerated and effeminate speech, *camp* may have had its origins in the dense living arrangements of young actors, many of them gay, who banded together in "gypsy camps" for economic reasons during the Great Depression. Today, it refers to almost any kind of haughty, hyperbolic innuendo, or even to an inclination towards the outrageous in clothing and furniture. "Camping" may seem (and often is) superficial and innocuous, but it can acquire a biting edge and evolve quickly into sarcasm. Although quick wit is a characteristic of the gay ghetto, not all gays are comfortable being "campy" because of the aura of the effeminacy and superficiality surrounding it.

Butch, an old term for "masculine" or *macho* has long since been taken over by chic straights. Its correlative, *nelly*, meaning effeminate or "swishy," is not as common. *S & M* means sado-masochistic — in this context, homosexual (or heterosexual) activities that involve inflicting or submitting to symbolic or actual physical pain or violence during sexual experience. *Chicken* means young, particularly someone (usually male) who is legally underage or looks it.

Among lesbians, the term *wimmin* represents a feminist attempt to remind both gay and straight men that they have their own culture and rituals, different from those of men.

Gay and lesbian jargon employs dozens of other phrases to designate people, behavior, dress, attitudes, relationships, and much more, most of which is either self-explanatory or not immediately relevant here. The special language of the ghetto serves many purposes: it ties people together verbally, almost as if by code, often in the form of double-meanings and connotations conveying subtle shades of meaning only other gay men or women would understand or appreciate. It has also served as an instrument of verbal exclusion against straights.

Of course the straight world also has its share of gay references — most of them highly pejorative: homo, queer, fairy, les, lesbo, faggot, fag, pansy, dyke, fruit, punk, poof, bugger, etc. Some of these terms were probably gay jargon at one time. Occasionally gays still use them, much as Blacks sometimes call each other "nigger" in a mildly censorious manner. But also like Blacks, gays understandably resent such terms when directed at them by outsiders. But gays use few words to express the same kind of contempt, ridicule, or antagonism toward straights as those listed above, or such as the Black term "whitey" manifests (the closest I have yet heard is "breeders"). This may well indicate a far greater interest in, as well as a fear of, homosexuality on the part of heterosexual people than most would care to admit to, as well as a curious lack of anti-straight sentiment among gays.

THE INVISIBLE WALL

As a more or less visible subculture, the gay world functions primarily as a commercial and social network, materialized in the form of several specifically gay institutions — gay or lesbian bars, bookstores, theaters, and arcades specializing in a wide variety of gay literature, including a range of soft to hard-core pornography. Gay brothels or "baths" have a long history. There are, as well, gay restaurants, clubs, discos, barber shops, health clinics, counseling centers, service organizations, newspaper offices, political headquarters, clothing stores, and churches. In addition, gay-owned establishments in the straight world, from art boutiques to haberdasheries, are often given preferential patronage. As a whole, the network is linked together by means of magazines, newspapers, newsletters, handouts, films, paperback books, and the ubiquitous "grapevine."

Except for the baths (now greatly reduced in numbers and popularity because of the fear of contracting AIDS in them), what is truly distinctive about ghetto institutions is not so much their goods and services, but their clientele, which tends to be exclusively gay and usually male. The lesbian ghetto is neither as extensive nor as public as its male counterpart. Some of the reasons for this include the greater overt persecution of gay men and, hence, the greater need for defensive association; the greater freedom of movement men traditionally enjoy in our culture; the greater wealth accessible to men; and the apparent preference of lesbians for private and domestic rather than public association. The sexual attraction that tends to bring men and women together in straight society is lacking, of course, in the gay world, which increases the separateness of the gay and lesbian ghettos, although gay and lesbian friendships are not uncommon.

In the past, the lesbian and gay ghettos overlapped only at the fringes. Today, greater political awareness and social solidarity among both groups encourage more exchange. In particular, the growth of compassion as a result of the AIDS epidemic as well as the continuing struggle for human liberation has fostered gay-lesbian association. Building community on such foundations presents a unique opportunity for the emergence of inter-sexual relationships of an especially important character today: non-erotic friendships. The quest for sexual satisfaction is by no means the only glue holding the gay world together internally.

At present, however, the gay world is predominantly a male-dominated one, perhaps even more than is the straight world. Thus, most of what I have to say about gay institutions applies primarily, if not solely, to those catering to men. Some male institutions, such as the baths, are totally absent from the lesbian world, as far as I know.

Not all urban gays, in fact only a small minority, actually live in the gay ghetto, whether that is considered to be a territory or a culturally closed realm of shared interests and values, etc. The ghetto is nevertheless the nucleus of the gay world, to a greater or lesser degree shaping the attitudes of most gays, even those who live in suburban and rural areas. Communication and travel are effective bonding agencies. Gay directories and bar guides provide access to gay areas of every major and many minor cities on a world-wide basis.

The gay social network was established in the pre-Stonewall era by benevolent organizations such as One, Inc., the Daughters of Bilitis, and the Mattachine Society. Today, political caucuses, service, professional, and ethnic associations, religious organizations, as well as various gay task forces, liberation groups, and a host of alliances reinforce this extensive, even international community in many different ways.[2]

GAY BARS

Most homosexual persons — about nine out of ten, according to some studies — have never seen the inside of one, but the gay bar has become the institutional symbol of the ghetto as the major recreational and social institution.[3] So successful are the bars, at least on a temporary basis, that in larger cities "superbars" draw not only gay crowds in the hundreds, but almost as many straight customers eager to capitalize on a comparatively safe variety of "radical chic." A city the size of Los Angeles, New York, or Chicago can support several "superbars" and as many as one hundred or more regular gay bars.

Most are pleasant-enough places, at least more so than the

majority of straight and even "singles" bars — less violent, more congenial, livelier, and in better repair. Many have restaurants and discos attached. Some are intentionally raunchy, some syndicate-owned, others discriminate against straights or even other gays, depending on whether a bar caters to lesbians, the S & M crowd, "cowboys," Blacks, Puerto Ricans, yuppies, or just males. In the 1980s, "video bars" featuring the latest rock and comedy videos televised on huge screens began to replace discos. (They have now become an institution in the straight world as well.) Lesbian bars tend to be smaller and less elaborate than male bars, partly because fewer lesbians "make the bar scene," and partly because the real money and power in the gay world are still in male hands.

Socially, the main function of the gay bar is to provide an open environment for drinking, mixing, cruising, sometimes dancing, and other forms of entertainment. But despite the positive contributions gay bars make to the lives of men and women who are often alone and lonely, they are first of all *bars*. As a result, they contribute to the serious problem alcoholism has become for many gay men and women. Bars are also money-making enterprises, of course, and they can be expensive meeting places, like any other commercial establishment. Further, despite the recreational benefits bars provide, they are intended to be cruising grounds and thus contribute their share to the sexual obsessiveness and promiscuity that tend to characterize the public gay world. The pressure exerted by the dynamics of the bar scene to appear young and attractive, the demands of sexual competition, coupled with inevitable frustrations, rejection, and l oneliness, all make the bars a highly mixed bag for gays searching for a life-style of integrity and dignity.

Since 1983 the threat of AIDS has reduced the level of promiscuity in the gay world to some extent, affecting bars in various ways. Many couples, whether lovers or friends, come to the bars simply to socialize. The majority of single customers leave alone. And despite their sometimes detrimental impact, it seems to me that bars are still one of the least harmful institutions in the gay world. As bars, I might add, they are usually cleaner, friendlier, and less expensive than equivalent straight establishments. In this respect, the gay world has probably had a redeeming effect on one of society's more troublesome institutions.

THE BATHS

Gay steam baths ("the tubs") were once an integral part of the male ghetto, whether the side attraction of run-down hotels catering to transients, or plush clubs featuring cafes, live entertainment, saunas, massage, swimming pools, gyms, and cocktail lounges. But in either case, the purpose of the baths was the same: to provide a safe arena for casual sexual encounters. Their popularity soon spread to the straight world, where there may now be more bath houses than in the gay ghetto, especially since New York, San Francisco, and other cities have closed gay baths in view of the AIDS epidemic.

With the advent of AIDS, it soon became evident to health authorities and even to many gay activists that the overt promiscuity the baths promoted also promoted the spread of disease. This was always the case with "curable" infections such as gonorrhea, herpes, and syphilis, not to mention mononucleosis, hepatitis, and the common cold. But the lethal aspect of AIDS quickly sobered the gay world to critical health issues once overlooked with insouciance and the availability of antibiotics.

Even apart from AIDS, from a Christian viewpoint today's baths are as detrimental to responsible sexuality as were those of the late Roman empire regardless of their harmless, even positive features. I shall return later to the problems created for a Christian spirituality by some of the exploitative institutions which debilitate the gay ghetto from within. It is worth noting here, however, that there are worse things both in the gay world and outside of it than bars and baths. At least they have provided a relatively humane escape for the lonely, frustrated, and rejected, as well as the compulsive, timid, and unattractive, and in this regard both institutions have had real social value. But in terms of human values such as intimacy, fidelity, and care, the baths in particular can never be more than a temporary palliative for loneliness and desire. The real problem, one ultimately of tragic proportions, lies in the fact that there were (and are) so few alternatives.

THE BUSHES AND BEACHES

Certain areas in cities and larger towns are generally well known by gays and many straights as cruising grounds — parks, stretches of beach, certain streets and parts of town, as well as railroad and subway stations, airports and bus terminals, where the public lavatories often provide available if risky points of rendezvous. Even in small towns, there is usually a "strip" where hustlers congregate, at least until police vigilance forces a relocation. In rural areas, there are gay taverns, as a rule not too far from major highways and usually known to interested parties in the general region. In small communities, individual gay homeowners may open their houses for meetings and parties.

Cruising the beaches and bushes is risky business, not merely because solicitation is illegal. Chance meetings often terminate in violence, occasionally even murder, as young hoodlums, desperate for drugs, liquor, or just money, prey on men equally desperate for clandestine sex. Hustlers themselves as well as unwary young gays out for a "trick" are sometimes attacked and even killed by psychopathic clients who suddenly vent their self-hatred on the previous object of their demented lust. This was borne out with horrifying clarity with the discovery of the predatory murders by John Wayne Gacy at Christmastide, 1978, and the sensational trial that followed. (Gacy, a married man accepted as heterosexual by his wife and associates, presents a classic if extreme example of the damage done to individuals and society by ignorance, sexual oppression, and the resistance of ordinary people to deal adequately with the fact of sexual variability.) Not the least risk of casual sexual escapades is contracting AIDS or another serious disease, forms of which are pandemic in the gay world.

Beyond the physical dangers, there are also the elements of psychological exploitation and spiritual degradation that render the bushes and beaches dangerous haunts for anyone who truly values self-respect and love. The continued existence of such "erogenous zones" constitutes an indictment of the social pressures that created and support them. (Dr. Martin Hoffman's now-classic study of the social factors giving rise to oppressive institutions in the gay world is still a valid and prophetic study of the "creation of social evil."[4])

EXTRA ADDED ATTRACTIONS

Lesser if not unimportant institutions in the lives of many gays include movie theaters and night clubs where drag shows and female impersonators are featured, bookstores and cheap arcades, and, beyond the geographical sphere, a variety of newspapers and magazines. While such diversions are by no means limited to gay audiences, especially the drag shows (long a major tourist attraction in New Orleans and San Francisco), the common element in most of them is more or less obvious pornography — the blatant exhibition and glorification of genital experience in all its forms, perhaps save only those of love, tenderness, and fidelity.

"Porno" films in particular have so little redeeming value of any kind, *especially* artistic, that it is difficult to see in them anything but voyeuristic avenues of escapism and mindless visual prostitution. Such "entertainments" are hardly restricted to a gay clientele, of course; most pornography panders to heterosexual tastes.

CREATIVE ALTERNATIVES

Gay liberation groups, church organizations, and associations such as the Mattachine Society, which have their special place in the history of the gay world, have criticized and sometimes even protested against the exploitative institutions in the ghetto, which is hardly coextensive with the gay world. They have also attempted to develop alternatives to the bars, bushes, and baths. Sports groups, bridge clubs, theater parties, discussion groups, picnics, tours and charter travel, dances, banquets, and other creative and enjoyable activities have been sponsored and are usually well-attended, especially by those who find the bars unappealing.

While temporary by nature and less obviously successful than their competition, such optional activities are needed in the gay world not only for what they are not, but because of the wider experience, educational input, and creative outlets they provide, enriching the gay community as a whole. As social acceptance increases and the need for protective association diminishes, such alternatives will become even more important in terms of enhancing the solidarity and stability of the gay world. But despite the fear and toll of AIDS, venereal and other diseases, alcoholism, drug abuse, and exploitation, we may expect that the bars, baths, and bushes will survive, and with them the drag balls and "beauty contests" that contribute towards the unattractive portrait of homosexual culture that persists in the mental vision of the straight population.

THE GAY WORLD

Overall, gay society is a sieve of gossip and rumor, punctuated by jealousies, envy, spite, callousness, schemes for petty revenge, sarcasm, fickleness, deceit, disloyalty, promiscuity, shallowness, and sometimes violence. It is a world dominated by tight conventions, custom, and style in everything from apparel, cosmetics, and hair to rituals of dance, new drinks, and topics of idle conversation. Outsiders are not usually welcome. Underlying everything are the subtle or gross patterns of mating games.

In short, the gay world is significantly like the straight world, from small town Peyton Places to suburban and metropolitan communities bound together by human weakness, sin, and culpability as much as by bonds of support, cooperation, and celebration. Not just a subculture, the gay world is also a microcosm of society as a whole, merely manifesting in sharper relief the vices and virtues of the dominant culture, minus much of the bland in-between.

As a condensation of the wider society, the gay world is also abundantly rich in important human values — intense loyalty, lasting friendships, trust, optimism, and collaboration. Genuine love and companionship are not lacking, nor are humor and depth. But many critics and even sympathetic observers fail to detect the positive side of gay life because they are more distracted than gays themselves by the surface sexual tension and campiness evident in many public gay haunts and habitats. Of course, gay men and women themselves can become insensitive to the unpromising and destructive aspects of gay life by reason of familiarity.

The dangers in the gay ghetto are the price of the ghetto itself. The overall problem is engulfment — being smothered by a preoccupation with homosexuality and the consequent loss of contact with the straight world. Gays run a real risk of becoming insensitive to the values, life-struggles, and needs of the great majority of people in the world by too exclusive a concentration on their own, thus reproducing the blindness that has prevented straight society from accepting gays all along.

But it is likewise important to recognize the positive functions of the gay ghetto — as a barricade against the depersonalization and loneliness many gays find in the straight world where they live and work and move, and as an environment which permits honesty and openness, mutual acceptance, and the opportunity for real friendships, some of life-long duration.

Gay Nemesis: The Specter of Aids

Since 1982, a cloud of anxiety and desperation has lowered over the gay world, its grim shadow reaching into every niche and nook of the ghetto and far beyond into the larger society and the remotest corners of the globe. Now a common household term, the Acquired Immune Deficiency Syndrome was unknown until 1981, when health authorities became concerned over the high incidence of rarely occurring but potentially lethal illnesses (called "opportunistic" infections) appearing among young gay men and Haitians in New York, Miami, Montreal, and San Francisco. Similar, even more virulent outbreaks were occurring in tropical Africa, Haiti, and Brazil among the heterosexual population.

Apparently, the first known blood samples infected with the AIDS virus were taken in 1959, in Kinshasa, Zaire. Why the virus became particularly infectious among homosexual males in North America and Europe remains a mystery, one that may never be solved. In 1982, medical researchers in America and France began a methodical but also maddeningly slow investigation, discovering the identity of the virus only some three years later. By then, hundreds of thousands of gay and bisexual men (as well as their male and female partners), Haitians, donated blood recipients, organ transplant recipients, intravenous drug users, and hemophiliacs had been exposed to the virus, which was transmitted through the blood system. By mid-1987, over forty thousand gay men had contracted serious diseases as a result of the collapse of their immune systems, and perhaps millions of non-gay persons had been exposed to the virus. Of the forty-five thousand total who had developed the largely fatal syndrome of diseases most people simply refer to now as AIDS, some twenty thousand had died.

The source of the AIDS virus remains obscure. For a time, Soviet authorities claimed that the virus resulted from American germ-warfare experiments. Similar charges were fired back. The virus may even have originated in a medical accident. Documented evidence shows the presence of an apparently "harmless" form of a retrovirus known as HTLV-3 (T-cell leukemia-lymphoma virus type three, more commonly known as HIV and, in France, LAV), or at least its antibodies, present in tropical Africa (Uganda, Zaire, and Kenya) in the

early 1970s.⁵ (A similar virus is found in fish off the coast of
Japan, where people have long since developed an antibody
indicating not only exposure but immunity to the virus. The
opposite seems to be the case with the HIV virus, the presence of
the antibody being taken to indicate that person exposed is now
a carrier rather than immune to the virus.)

A report published in the London *Times* on May 11, 1987,
suggested that the intensive smallpox inoculation program of
the World Health Organization may have inadvertently
instigated a mutation of the innocuous African virus into the
deadly form which produced AIDS. (The disease is now
epidemic in Eastern Africa and inexorably spreading westward.)
Brazil, which was also part of the WHO smallpox eradication
effort, now shows the highest incidence of AIDS in South
America. Haiti, where AIDS is also unusually widespread,
may have been indirectly affected when 14,000 Haitians were
vaccinated in South Africa before returning home in the middle-
to-late 'seventies. (AIDS was unknown in Haiti before 1978.)
It has also been conjectured that infected mercenaries returning
from Angola transmitted the disease to Haiti when they
stopped off there en route to Cuba. Other medical researchers
claim that the AIDS virus did not originate in Africa, but was
introduced there about the same time that it appeared in the
United States and elsewhere.⁶ Recent reports suggest that
undiagnosed cases of AIDS appeared in the United States and
England as early as 1969.

Wherever the virus developed and however it spread, it
works insidiously, attacking and destroying the white blood
cells that enable the immune system to ward off infections. The
syndrome appears in two stages, the first marked by fever,
swollen lymph glands, upper respiratory infections, canker
sores, a painless white patch known as "hairy leukoplakia" on
the tongue, chronic diarrhea, exhaustion, and especially marked
loss of weight. The second, lethal phase of the disease results
from the suppression of the immune system caused by the
invading virus, which permits opportunistic infections to occur.
Most serious among them are a rare form of blood vessel cancer

called Kaposi's Sarcoma (abbreviated KS), and an equally rare form of pneumonia known as pneumocystis carinii (or PCP). The virus can also enter the central nervous system and damage both nerves and the brain itself, producing pronounced personality changes and mental impairment.

At present, infection by the AIDS virus is incurable and, according to some reports, invariably fatal once the opportunistic diseases develop. This may or may not be true; a number of PWAs (Persons with AIDS) have survived for as long as seven years, longer than the length of time the virus has been known. It is also too soon to tell whether every person exposed to the virus and showing positive evidence of antibodies will develop the full-blown syndrome of diseases. Various drugs are also slowly coming into use which retard or alleviate the symptoms of AIDS. But a true vaccine is not expected to be perfected for several more years.

A Human Tragedy

In the U.S., the first notable instances of AIDS appeared in California and New York where large numbers of gay men and women have congregated for over a decade. It has been conjectured that gays vacationing in Haiti were exposed to the virus there and transmitted it to the ghettos on their return. In North America, about three-fourths of all AIDS cases involve homosexual men, a fact which gave rise to the myth that AIDS was a "gay disease."

As the "gay plague" devastated the ghettos of New York, Los Angeles, and San Francisco, desperation and panic began to spread. Soon, however, it became apparent that AIDS was not a gay disease, but a disease that affected gay men as well as others, including heterosexual men and women, the elderly, children, and was even transmitted to infants in the womb if their mothers were exposed. In Africa and other areas, AIDS strikes predominantly among heterosexual men and women. But AIDS has also been contracted by drug users sharing contaminated needles, hemophiliacs, and recipients of blood donations and organ transplants. It has been acquired very rarely by health workers who tend to AIDS patients but who were careless about cuts or abrasions on their own bodies.

AIDS cannot be transmitted by ordinary human interaction, however. Sharing food utensils, plates, clothing, toilet facilities, or even coming into direct physical contact with someone having AIDS will not transmit the virus, which cannot survive in air. In this respect, AIDS is not contagious, but "infectious." To quarantine persons with AIDS is therefore not only an inhumanly cruel act, it is also unnecessary.

AVOIDING AIDS

Sexual intercourse (especially with strangers), whether vaginal or anal, and intravenous drug-use remain the major avenues of infection for homosexual, bisexual, and heterosexual persons. The route of infection is invariably through the blood stream. It is therefore not only possible but easy to avoid contracting AIDS, especially by abstaining from sexual intercourse with carriers of the virus, as well as avoiding intravenous drug use. (Blood products and organ transplants are now carefully screened to prevent contamination.)

For those who are unwilling or unable to remain sexually abstinent or free from drug use, using condoms and refusing to share hypodermic needles with other drug-users will significantly reduce (but not eliminate) the risk of AIDS. It is extremely important to bear in mind that even if a vaccine becomes available, there is no known antidote to AIDS once contracted. The hundreds of thousands of persons already stricken by the virus, and the millions more who may be, will therefore require both medical and spiritual assistance as they undergo the ordeal of advancing illness and perhaps death from painful, often disfiguring diseases.

MINISTRY

Contrary to the fulminations of religious bigots, AIDS is no more a sign of the so-called "wrath of God" towards homosexuality than towards heterosexuality, hemophilia, blood recipients, intravenous drug users, or fetuses. It can and does reveal, however, people's "habits of the heart" (including those of professional religious leaders), such as their notion of God. AIDS questions us all as to whether the God we worship is a God of love, mercy, and compassion who calls us to manifest the same qualities towards the sick, imprisoned, oppressed, and homeless (see Mt 25:31ff.), or a vengeful deity who visits disease and disaster on the innocent and delights in the death of sinners. Moral theologian Fr. Bernard Häring observes in this regard, "The fate of those with AIDS, both those who acted irresponsibly and those who caught it without any personal fault, is one of the signs of the times calling us to a radical conversion."[7]

Despite the spiteful remarks of the self-righteous, the onslaught of the AIDS epidemic has evoked a heroically generous spirit in both the gay and straight communities. Volunteer associations such as Shanti in San Francisco have grown into full-time ministries providing care, companionship, and assistance to persons with AIDS in hospitals, hospices, and their own homes. In many instances, gay service centers have stretched themselves beyond their limits to provide assistance. Similarly, many religious denominations, dioceses, and orders, as well as state and private organizations have inaugurated educational and training programs for AIDS counselors. Many have set up hospices and donated services.

Still, it is not enough. Such programs can only barely meet the most serious situations, largely those involving persons with AIDS who have exhausted their resources and have no one to whom to turn. Still needing support, educational resources, and contacts are millions of persons who have tested positive for the virus but show no signs of disease, as well as persons with AIDS-related diseases, and the wives, husbands, lovers, children, parents, relatives, co-workers, and friends of those who have contracted AIDS itself or one of its lesser forms.

AIDS is not only a challenge common to the medical field, social workers, and organized religion. It is even more than a general invitation to compassion and care. It is a command, a divine summons to each of us, a call to ministry.

NOTES

1. Cf. the Statement by the Catholic Bishops of England and Wales, op. cit., p. 7: "With regard to homosexual acts, scripture and the on-going tradition of Christianity make it quite clear that these are immoral. Whatever pastoral judgement may conclude concerning personal responsibility in a particular case, it is clear that in the objective order homosexual acts may not be approved."
2. A brief list of major service and religious organizations can be found in Resources for Further Reading below, pp. 181ff.
3. Cf. Wayne Sage, "Inside the Colossal Closet," *Human Behavior* 4, 8 (August 1975): 16ff.
4. Martin Hoffman, *The Gay World: The Social Creation of Evil*, New York: Bantam, 1969.
5. Cf. Eileen Flynn, *AIDS: A Catholic Call for Compassion*, Kansas City: Sheed and Ward, 1985, p. 19.
6. Cf. R. Sher, M.B., et al., "Seroepidemiology of Human Immunodeficiency Virus in Africa from 1970 to 1974," *New England Journal of Medicine* 317,7 (August 13, 1987): 450-51. I am endebted to Dr. Herbert Ratner for this reference.
7. "A Call to Radical Conversion," in Cosstick, *AIDS: Meeting the Community Challenge*, ed. cit., p. 89. Earlier, Häring remarks, "Faced with those who suffer from AIDS, we should remind ourselves of the warning of Jesus: 'Judge not, that you be not judged' (Mt. 7:1). We will abstain from a judgmental attitude towards those who are affected by the AIDS virus when we realize how deeply AIDS is embedded in our sick culture, through our own co-operation in it. Can we really dare to say that we are immune from all those attitudes which spread unhealthiness and increase the risks inherent in unhealthy relationships – a judgmental attitude being one of them?" (p. 88).

CHAPTER FIVE

Gay Life Journeys

THE social structures of the gay world exert considerable pressure on gay men and women to conform to the expected patterns of participation in it. While some of these patterns of thought, value, and behavior can be destructive, as in any social system, these same structures also create the possibility for the association and solidarity necessary for psychological and spiritual integrity among a minority group of any kind.

Three transition periods in a gay person's life stand out as particularly important regarding all these structures and pressures as well as the opportunities and problems they present: coming out, the crisis period, and aging.

COMING OUT

The ability to recognize and accept one's homosexuality and to share that discovery with others marks a transition or "rite of passage" from the officially straight world to the gay world. For many young lesbians and gay men, the transition is easier today than a generation ago because of the greater receptiveness of their families and friends. For others, coming out is a crucifixion which can create disaster for family relations and elicit rejection from friends and acquaintances alike. Knowing this, some gays understandably but unfortunately never "get around" to telling even their closest friends and relatives about themselves. This means, in turn, that their social lives will span two worlds, with the continual possibility and therefore fear of discovery and mutual hurt.

Much more than a merely historical moment in a person's life journey, coming out is a psychological and spiritual achievement. For many, it is akin to a religious conversion.[1] Once "out," they experience a tremendous sense of relief and well-being, a conviction of honesty, and an exhilarating feeling of freedom. Frequently, however, the exuberance is short-lived, especially if coming out is associated with a deep plunge into the whirlpool of sexual adventures open especially to the young. Sometimes a reaction of intense depression follows, coupled with a sense of loss and the fear that there is no going back but also little by way of a future. Some highly sensitive teenagers and older gay men and lesbians as well may even attempt suicide at this time, particularly when there has been a hurtful experience of familial rejection.

Not all gays come out as teenagers; most perhaps come out in their twenties and thirties, after college, or as they take up a place in the work-a-day world. Some come out in middle or even old age, others after a marriage failure, others after the death of a spouse. In each case, coming out has its own character, whether easy and thrilling, slow and uneventful, or difficult and, later on, regrettable. That vast majority of gays never get all the way out of the closet, by the way. Their reasons are usually good ones; not everyone who resists being labeled does so out of fear. Coming out has problems associated with it that are not wholly the effect of a traditionally hostile society, but stem from the fact of being labeled itself, whether by oneself or by others. I shall return to the problem of labeling; here, it is enough to point out an important difference between being recognized and accepted as gay and the public proclamation of that fact.

If you are gay, from a psychological and spiritual perspective, coming out in the basic sense of self-acceptance and openness with significant others should be a constructive move, provided that you have sufficient inner strength and social support to carry through successfully. A half-hearted, experimental "try" can be permanently damaging to your own self-esteem and to your reputation among family members and associates.

Coming out without sufficient self-acceptance is an invitation to further problems. Needless to add, self-acceptance is not achieved in a single stroke of affirmation — it is a life-long process. By *sufficient* self-acceptance, I mean a fundamental sense of self-worth that can provide enough psychological stamina for you to endure rather severe challenges and opposition. From a religious point of view, it means a basic conviction that you are deeply known and infinitely loved by God just as you are, and that you are following the route your conscience approves as your way to Christian maturity and lasting self-respect. It involves a willingness to be proved wrong, knowing that you can always do better and that a mistake need never be terminal. In this respect, coming out must be a part of your "fundamental option" for ultimate integrity and well-being as a friend of man, woman, and God.

Before coming out, then, *be sure you're gay!* Today college and even high school experience provides ample opportunity for sexual experimentation. As a consequence, many young men and women may have as many or even more homosexual as heterosexual encounters, but without being thereby ready to or even capable of coming out for the simple reason that they are not really gay.

Among adolescents, considerable activity goes on which may be technically homosexual but does not indicate constitutional homosexuality, much less pathology or even grave immorality. I am referring to behavior such as initiation rituals or hazing in clubs, fraternities, and sororities, as well as "circle jerks," and other forms of mutual masturbation or simply the mutual exploration that goes on among children.

Some youngsters who participate in same-sex games will eventually come out gay, but others, most others, will not. This is no indication that the first group is "fixated," or that the second is "latent" — conditions that are both highly mythological. Counselors especially should be alert to the *variety* of possible directions sexual orientation may take in a young person's life;

experiences at any one period of development cannot be taken as representative of the entire process nor indicative of the outcome. Sexual identity is not complete, in all likelihood, until the middle twenties, even though most gay and straight adolescents will be well aware of the predominant direction of their sexual interests by the time they are sixteen or seventeen. Some kinds of sexual experimentation, including homosexual experiences, must therefore be considered as falling within the normal range of adolescent behavior. The morality of such behavior must be judged accordingly.

To repeat, *the capacity to respond sexually to a person of the same gender is not equivalent to being homosexual.* In this sense, *gay* means the recognition and acceptance of a predominant sexual attraction to persons of the same gender with a proportionate and constitutional lack of attraction to members of the opposite gender. The number of men and women who have had homosexual "experiences" but have gone on to happy and successful lives as husbands, wives and parents *far outweighs* the number whose sexual preference and experience are predominantly or exclusively gay or straight. Integrating such experiences into a balanced sexual history can contribute to human wholeness; denying them, trying to "forget" them, or worrying about them for years merely present occasions for needles self-deprecation.

Similarly, given the fundamental homosexual *capacity* in every one of us, the emergence in consciousness of homosexual attraction or even genital arousal should not be an occasion for panic. It is likely that most straight men and women will sometimes experience strong attractions like these, even after marriage. Neither panic, flight, nor a total capitulation to homosexual infatuation are mature responses. But if the situation is met adequately, that is with honesty and restraint, greater self-awareness and the growth of valuable and lasting relationships will most likely result.

In a word, all of us are more or less bisexual, even though the homosexual component of our personalities may never figure prominently in either consciousness or behavior. On the other hand, for a husband or wife who experiences recurrent homosexual "crushes," fantasies, or finds herself or himself actively involved in a homosexual affair, skilled counseling is probably warranted. If a professional counselor is unavailable, talking things over calmly with one's spouse, an understanding pastor or trusted friend *may* help. But resolutely hiding the situation will not. Bisexuality need not destroy a marriage, provided that both partners are able to cope with the situation maturely. Making a marriage successful in such a situation requires immense dedication, love, and discipline. But it can be done.

Both research and pastoral experience indicate that the number of bisexual and homosexual men and women in heterosexual marriages is much higher than might be expected, a fact tragically borne out with regard to the number of heterosexual women who have contracted AIDS from a spouse or lover. Perhaps even a majority of the actual homosexual population is married. A priests' survey conducted for the Thomas More Association in 1977 indicated that 35 percent of those asking for pastoral help for a homosexual problem were married; 24 percent had children.[2]

Attempting to generalize from the experience of troubled persons tends to unbalance the issue on the side of the sickness and tragedy — as seen in the work of many psychiatrists and counselors such as the otherwise sympathetic treatment of Fr. Marc Oraison.[3] One important conclusion that may be drawn legitimately from such a survey seems to be that, despite problems, heterosexual marriage and some degree of homosexuality are not absolutely incompatible. Further, many of these marriages would be considered successful by ordinary standards of evaluation in our society. On the other hand, many homosexual men and women feel trapped in marriages by the force of social and religious pressure and are, in fact, living a lie. Honesty, justice, and plain mental health call for a serious and sincere confrontation in such cases, and even the dissolution or annulment of the marriage.

At present, few counselors in high school or college, much

less the family doctor or minister, are sufficiently skilled to aid a young person or an older one in resolving problems of sexual orientation. At the minimum, it is crucial to find an advisor who is neither prejudiced against homosexuality as such nor a gay propagandist. Responsible counseling services, some of which specialize in sexual identity crises, can be located through referral by organizations such as the National Gay and Lesbian Task Force, and local resources including community service organizations and religious groups such as Dignity, Integrity, the Metropolitan Community Church, Lutherans Concerned, etc. (For addresses of national resource groups, see the Resources for Further Study at the end of this book.)

Ideally, coming out should be achieved in the context of a well-integrated relationship with those with whom you choose to share this important part of your life. For most gays, especially the young, there will be a desire to share the fact of their gayness with close friends and especially with their families. Older gays frequently want to include their close business associates or co-workers — an important step in so far as work relationships today are often some of the most significant in our lives. It may well be that they wish to include their pastor, doctor, lawyer, and other personal associates. Some will want to tell the world.

Here, common sense, courtesy, and compassion will have to figure. Not everyone is likely to be ready for your announcement as soon as you are. The wider the intended audience, the greater the risk of misunderstanding and rejection, as well as other repercussions. If you are gay and considering coming out, you should judge each situation according to its own merits and context, and not merely in terms of your desire to be open. Enthusiasm can easily engender insensitivity.

However you decide to announce your gayness, concern for others as well as sincere self-respect ought to guide the announcement. If you have had the good fortune to receive counsel from an understanding minister, teacher, or other trusted mentor, it may well help to have him or her present when you meet with your parents (or children, wife or husband). Other situations must be handled with similar care. Generally, when dealing with friends and acquaintances outside the immediate family group, it is wise to work from a foundation of achieved — not *presumed* — trust and respect. Premature self-disclosure can prohibit further opportunities for acceptance and mutual growth. Coming out aggressively, whether to punish, retaliate against, or to wound someone either in anger or, as is often the case, in pain, is at best childish, and more likely to be both manipulative and cruel. The slogan and toilet-wall graffito "My mother made me gay" is probably false and at best a gross oversimplification, but vastly effective as a weapon to demolish a parent already anxious about her "mistake" in child-rearing. Coming out, if used to exonerate oneself and incriminate others is evidence of a precarious attitude. Simply speaking, it is a cop-out: "See what you made me do?"

Parents, friends, relatives, and co-workers of a gay person may often need more help to adjust than the gay "debutante" herself or himself. Having a gay daughter or son is taken to be a sign of personal failure; many close friends seem to fear guilt by association or even being "contaminated" — in both the metaphorical and, with so much mis-information around about AIDS, the literal sense. Compassion and a better knowledge of the health in homosexuality should make such fears decrease, but they will probably never vanish, so long as human beings remain as mysterious and threatening to themselves as they are to each other.

If *your* child or parent, spouse or friend wishes to tell you that he or she is gay, be aware that this is an expression of confidence and trust from a person whose felt needs and vulnerability are at least as acute as yours, and who needs your respect, love, and support more than anything in the world at that moment. Coming out should not be a personal disaster for anyone, nor a family crisis filled with scenes of self-recrimination and accusation. All things considered, everyone is better off when lesbians and gays are comfortably out of their restrictive identity-closets and accepted — not coddled, pitied, or even tolerated (which is demeaning and patronizing) — just *accepted*.

COMING OUT PUBLICLY

Self-acceptance and acceptance by others in a person's immediate circle of family and friends are not *enough*, of course, to build a life on. Nevertheless, they are the necessary foundation and therefore far more important than public declarations. Without such acceptance as a foundation of support, public identification can be a very risky venture into the merciless social dynamics of labeling and "deviance." With genuine personal acceptance, public proclamations may even be unnecessary for many lesbians and gay men. Nevertheless, such political coming out often serves a positive purpose in changing general attitudes as well as exponentially raising the vital sense of self-worth among talented, constructively aggressive gay men and lesbians. Such a decision should remain a matter of individual choice, however, and not foisted on anyone against their better judgment. The real point of coming out is not to inform the straight world who is gay, but to secure a sense of valid personal identity and social integrity.

Many of the now-classic public utterances of liberated gays in the early 1970s — "Gay is good," "Gay Power!" and "Out of the closets, into the streets!" — called to mind the original slogans generated by the emergence of black power and the feminist movements: "I am somebody!" "Black is beautiful!" "Sisterhood is Powerful!" The startled and antagonistic reactions from the more conservative quarters in the political, psychological, and theological establishments which greeted these outbursts of "I'm OK" enthusiasm by men and women long conceded to be far from OK were also reminiscent of the uncomfortable response to the demand of Blacks, Native Americans, and women for recognition and greater participation in social life.

Whether true, mythical or just wishful thinking, the positive assertion of health, worth, and dignity on the part of gays, however exaggerated or rhetorical, was a necessary and constructive phase of the dialectic of acceptance. Such claims did not in themselves *constitute* health, much less acceptability, but they helped create conditions for gaining both in a highly effective way. They still can. Affirmative sloganeering becomes problematic only if, behind a screen of propaganda, they obscure to straights or gays themselves the depths of pain and struggle involved in being openly gay. Thus, regardless if the chant "Gay is good" set peoples' teeth on edge, and no matter how absurd the riders "Gay is better," "Gay is best," the fact remains that *gays* are good.

Although the campaign for greater social and religious acceptance of homosexual persons was in many respects successful in the 'seventies, set-backs occurred in the area of civil rights in the wake of the AIDS epidemic, especially with regard to housing and employment. (Gays and even lesbians were not the only people to find their rights threatened by their AIDS-fearing neighbors, however. This was especially sad in the case of children denied the right to public education, medical patients, and the wives and husbands of persons who had contracted AIDS medically.) As a result, it is much more difficult for gays and lesbians to be publicly "out." For that very reason, it may be even more important.

THE CRISIS PERIOD

Being young is probably valued more in the world of gay men and lesbians than in any other segment of society. Consequently, adolescence is typically extended to the utmost limits of credibility and aging is postponed (and feared) proportionately. Thus, the crisis period in the lives of many gays, especially men, is "the hump" — a period somewhere around thirty years of age, after which it becomes more and more difficult to pass as twenty-two or twenty-three, although many try.

Ironically, because of the higher premium placed on youth, good looks, and physical fitness, the "mid-years," with their crises of limits and transition phases, plus the need for self-redefinition in terms of personal and career opportunities, begin earlier in the gay world than in its straight counterpart. In both worlds, handsome, youthful men and attractive, slim young women have more to lose with the passing of youth than their less well-endowed peers. But since they lack the socially-approved refuge of marriage and family life open to heterosexual men and women, many gays cling much more feverishly to every vestige of youth, succumbing only resentfully to advancing maturity — with its threats of loneliness, wrinkles, grey hair (or no hair), loss of vitality, limited sociability, and the inevitable slowing towards old age and death.

As "middlescence" approaches, many lesbians seem especially tempted to "let go," meeting the so-called ravages of time with grim abandon rather than graceful acceptance. As with the aging male, lesbians at this period of life, particularly those who do not have a lover, need and should receive a great deal of support and encouragement — but not nagging or pampering. For in the difficult throes of this second radical challenge to self-affirmation, lesbians and gay men must themselves appropriate the positive values and goals that will bring meaning and satisfaction to the closing years of their lives.

Handling acute depression, which sometimes accompanies the physiological and psychological changes at this period of life for *both* men and women, requires expert assistance. Therapists insensitive to the unique needs of gays can do immeasurable harm by a mistaken attack on sexual orientation. And although skilled helpers sensitized to the special needs of gay people are still greatly lacking, they are slowly increasing in number and professional competence. Such gay "specialists" are, moreover, devoting greater attention to the dynamics of the mid-years crises and aging.

Middle age is a time of life for many gays when the confines of the gay ghetto become too narrow; one of life's great discoveries as a person matures is the potential of human fulfillment on levels of interest and enjoyment that transcend youthful preoccupations and sexual differences. Wider social and cultural activities become, therefore, especially rewarding as gays and lesbians cross over "the hump." Many break out of the ghetto at this point — one reason why older men and women are not conspicuous in the bars and a more positive one than the mere fact of being older.

Although there are many common elements in gay and straight experiences and relationships, communication, intimacy, and aging present particular stresses and problems for gays and lesbians. So, while gay persons can benefit greatly from counseling experiences, human relations workshops, and even books on personality development and interpersonal growth that are designed primarily for the straight world, there is a special need for gay counseling, seminars, and resources. In many larger urban areas, gay service organizations and religious groups provide personal growth opportunities through shared experiences conducted by trained supervisors.

AGING GAILY

Today, despite the fundamental and even necessary role in gay liberation of coming out and staying in one piece, they are only the beginning of a meaning-filled, creative, and developing life for gay men and women of every age. Especially after gays successfully surmount "the hump," they often begin to relax and to enjoy life more rather than less. Male gays in their forties and thereafter are more likely to follow the pattern of their lesbian sisters, find a lover, and "settle down." (The number of "unions" among male gays is much higher than the myth allows even many gays to believe; serial monogamy is more the rule than a permanent relationship with a single person, but lasting relationships are not uncommon, even among younger gays.) Most "aged" gays I know, far from being bitter, lonely and depressed, are remarkably contented men and women. Social research seems to be increasingly confirming this and similar observations.[4]   Older gays are often spared some of the more difficult trials of their straight counterparts — the disruption of the family group, the gradual loss of contact with children and grandchildren, finding oneself increasingly isolated and ignored with advancing age, or even relegated to a "home" and forgotten. For lovers, however, age brings its losses to both gays and straights alike — the gradual disappearance of friends, the inevitable loss of one's life-companion, the smaller diminishments of dwindling income, strength, and health.

Advanced age need not be a period of loneliness, even for single or "widowed" gays, however; the greater solidarity of the gay world provides social contacts and opportunities for sharing often denied straight persons. I have often been amazed and gratified to see the consideration and attention young gays show their elder brothers and sisters as well as their own aged parents and relatives. Older gays seem, as well, to acquire a sense of detachment not only from the gay world, but from the world in general which I cannot help but see as a religious response to the developing awareness of life's beauty and meaning. Nevertheless, they also preserve a sense of care and interest in people and the two worlds they live in that exceeds that of far younger people.

Increasingly, older gay men and lesbians are investing in community retirement complexes, especially but not exclusively in the "sun-belt" states. The proximity such joint ventures provide can contribute greatly to the social contacts helpful and even necessary for a fully rounded life and spiritual health in later years. SAGE, Inc. (Senior Action in a Gay Environment), is a New York-based community service organization that offers valuable assistance and social opportunities for older gay men and lesbians.[5] As a networking agency, SAGE has an extensive mailing list around the country and presents an effective model that could — and should — be imitated in larger metropolitan areas everywhere.

Throughout your life, if you are gay, it *is* possible to enjoy a sense of well-being and personal dignity that will bring you to the end of your days a happy and peaceful person, despite the many difficulties and setbacks that inevitably will come. Having met a good many elderly gays over the past six years, I can say that with some assurance, which I hope the parents and friends of gays will find encouraging. Successfully negotiating the perils of "the hump" and learning to relish the long slope down the other side of thirty requires discipline, however — the strenuous art of refusing to identify yourself with the surface realities of being gay, while affirming yourself as a loved and lovable person chosen by God for reasons both divine and mysterious to follow a life-way toward Home *as* a gay person.

BEYOND THE GHETTO

Except for a few novels, little has been written on the life situations of ordinary homosexual men and women who have only minor contact with the gay ghetto, much less its deviant fringe. This is mainly because so little is known even about the actual extent of homosexuality in our society. Alfred Kinsey's work in the 1950s broke the ground scientifically. Unfortunately, social research has not progressed very far since his pioneering studies because of the reluctance of the federal government to help finance studies of sexuality, especially those dealing with subjects felt to be politically dangerous. Private funding agencies are somewhat more willing to sponsor research, but very little work has yet been done. Almost nothing is known about the religious lives of ordinary gay people outside the visible gay community reached by groups such as Dignity, Integrity, the Metropolitan Community Church, and other church groups.

For instance, if a Dignity chapter reaches 300 Catholic gays in a city such as Chicago, it is *not* reaching the other 100,000 and probably never will. Nevertheless, the ministerial capacity of religious organizations in the gay community is truly enormous — and as a force for moral development and witness should not be underestimated on the basis of the unrepresentative size of its constituency. But what of the other ninety percent of the homosexual population who are not part of the manifest gay world, much less in contact with Dignity or MCC, and who for a variety of reasons will probably never come even part way out of their privacy and invisibility?

First of all, and most generally, being publicly "out" is not necessary or even possible for many homosexual men and women who might otherwise not only be comfortable with their gay orientation but also are known to be gay to a limited number of close friends and associates. It is important for *some* gays to be publicly visible, in order to provide adequate role models for other gays and to counteract the negative stereotype perpetuated by anti-gay opponents. But not all gays need be publicly visible — and, I think, not all *should* be. In fact, most gays are indistinguishable from anyone else — and since, as many gays insist, they *aren't* fundamentally different, their very invisibility is a sign of the normalcy of gay life. It should be remembered that most gays are invisible not only to the otherwise straight world, but also to the public gay world — especially the ghetto.

What then of the vast majority of gays who are not found in the bars, who do not go to the baths or prowl the bushes for quick and anonymous sexual adventure? What is the shape of their lives? What are their problems and hopes? What is likely to happen if they turn to a parish priest or counsellor for help in coping with their sexuality or other problematic areas of life? How do they feel about the Church? What does it mean to be a gay person in the Church?

GAY CHRISTIANS

As with most aspects of gay life outside the confines of the visible community — with its nuclear ghetto — we just don't know for the most part. As a result, my own limited attempts to fathom the meaning of gay experience in the Church, and Christian experience among gays, has led me only to some tentative conclusions. First, to be a gay Christian, and especially to be publicly known as such, is to be a witness to the Catholicity of Christianity at the leading edge of its truest humanity, that is, at the sexual level.

Christians have always been extremely sensitive to the sexual dimension of life — perhaps overly so, in contrast to Jesus' apparent attitude. Any deviation here has often been reckoned as an unforgivable sin — particularly so homosexuality. To be a gay Christian then, means requiring the Church to examine itself on an issue of profound importance. Today, more specifically, it means that the Church must not only advert to the distinction between the person and behavior, between the sinner and the sin, in traditional terms, but it must also reexamine its understanding of the limits of normal, healthy, and thus natural sexual behavior.

Perhaps even more importantly, to be a Christian gay also means that the gospel has penetrated visibly into the gay ghetto in some cases, or that it has at least reached the ears of those who have longed to hear of human liberation. It means that the sinful social structures of the gay world — and there are plenty, just as in straight society — will stand out in sharper relief, and no doubt that there will be a felt tension as a result. For a Christian gay to be indistinguishable in the ghetto means not to be Christian except in name. The redemption of the gay world is inaugurated by the *real* presence of men and women for whom the good news of liberation is not merely a passage read and celebrated on Sundays.

I have no doubts at this point that the insistence of gay Christians for recognition by the Church is a movement inspired by the Holy Spirit. Not every expression of that movement will be an adequate sign of that fact, and mistakes will be made. We are all unprofitable servants in the best of times — bishops and theologians, too. But ultimately, if I am correct, the Spirit of Catholic Christianity will prevail, despite our bumbling. In the meantime, great patience is needed, but great courage as well. We are learning new things about life and the world that will probably continue to shake us up for some time. But we should not attempt to run from the issues before us, for with this challenge, as with many others, *this* is the acceptable time, *this* is the day of salvation.

NOTES

1. See in this regard, James D. Whitehead and Evelyn Eaton Whitehead, *Christian Life Patterns*, Garden City, New York: Doubleday and Co., 1982; James D. Whitehead and Evelyn Eaton Whitehead, "Three Passages of Maturity," in Robert Nugent, SDS, ed., *A Challenge to Love*, New York: Crossroad, 1986, pp. 174-88; and James R. Zullo and James D. Whitehead, "The Christian Body and Homosexual Maturing," ibid., pp. 20-37.

2. Statistics compiled by the Thomas More Association, 223 W. Erie St., Chicago, Ill. 60610, for publication in the newsletter *For Priests*, March 1977, No. II.

3. Cf. *The Homosexual Question*, New York: Harper & Row, 1977. Oraison's treatment reflects his pronounced and somber existentialism as much as it does the fact that his experience has been admittedly limited to disturbed clients. Clinical practice among disturbed and unhappy homosexual patients has long influenced the writing of many therapists, whose experience with the healthy homosexual population (i.e., the great majority) appears to be very limited. Among such one-sided accounts I would include those of Walter C. Alvarez, Ruth Tiffany Barnhouse, Edmund Bergler, Irving Bieber, Fr. John Harvey, and Charles Socarides.

4. See especially Alan P. Bell and Martin S. Weinberg, *Homosexualities: A Study of Diversity among Men and Women*, op. cit. On aging, also see Karlen, op. cit., pp. 531-33 and especially Keith Vacha, *Quiet Fire: Memoirs of Older Gay Men*, ed. by Cassie Damewood, Trumansburg, NY: Crossing Press, 1985.

5. For the address, see Resources for Further Study below, pp. 181ff.

CHAPTER SIX

Living with the Church

"ABOUT a month ago, I went to the 'Winter Carnival' with a friend of mine. Saw the Dignity booth and both of us being Catholic walked over to it and picked up some literature. I suggested to my friend that we should go to 'St. Aelred's' some Sunday as it would be a 'decent place' to meet people. We finally went last Sunday....

"I had an unexpected surprise. We were trying to participate in the service. I was standing in church attempting to sing when all of a sudden I wanted to cry, it felt so good to be participating in a Mass again. I choked back the tears because I didn't want my friend to laugh at me. I had a good warm feeling inside me. I still do. I suppose I have returned to the Church or will more fully as time goes on. It's really strange — I went to church to meet people and I think I've been reintroduced to the One I least expected to meet. I went to Mass last night for the sake of going to Mass, not to meet people."

The experience of the thirty-six-year-old man who wrote these words is not a rare one among the many gay men and women who have "come back to the church" through the programs and witness of Dignity, the Metropolitan Community Church, Jewish congregations such as Los Angeles' Metropolitan Community Temple, and other groups. What is remarkable is that they do come back, given the traditional religious hostility toward gays and lesbians. Some, of course, never left: "I remained because of a firm background understanding of the message of love in the Gospel.... I was able with the help of a good advisor to distinguish between the letter and the spirit of the law." A woman of forty-six wrote, "I have remained within our church because of an understanding young priest at our parish." A man of fifty-one explained simply, "I have never left the church and have always remained in it because I don't think there is any better."

Despite some hostility and bitterness toward an institution traditionally opposed to any manifestation of homosexuality as contrary to God's law and nature itself, vast numbers of lesbians and gay men continue to revere the church and to desire to be full members — but not necessarily as celibates. Not a few church leaders are beginning to agree that they may have a case.

Practice has often departed from theory in the pastoral ministry as well as in the private lives of priests, ministers, popes, and rabbis. But for about the last thousand years, homosexuality has been considered a serious deterrent to a full religious life, if not an abomination worthy of death, by most western religious traditions. In England even as late as 1102, however, St. Anselm prevented the promulgation of anti-homosexual laws as being contrary to papal decree. At that time, the English church may not have considered homosexual acts gravely sinful.[1] But the more general practice of church ministers, at least officially, has been to ban and even burn offenders. Not the least of their harshness has been expressed in the penances dealt out in the confessional. A recent favorite of several confessors in one Chicago parish was requiring penitents to wash their mouths out in the urinal of a public lavatory in the church. (Having been told this on various occasions by at least a half-dozen different men, I am inclined to accept it as a true account, although at first I could not bring myself to believe it.)

While not a typical penance, similar atrocities have not been uncommon in the religious experience of gays. I have heard many accounts of psychological and even physical abuse, such as a confessor's shouting at a penitent in the confessional of a crowded church, or even pulling a teenager out of the "box" and striking him. A young man of twenty-six relates: "While on my high school retreat during my senior year, I told a priest about my being gay, although at the time I was not actually a practicing gay. He read me up one side and down the other, chewed me up and spit me out at much louder tones than a normal talking voice. When I walked back into the room, all heads turned and looked at me, or at least I thought so. That caused eight years' separation between the church and myself." Similarly, Protestant ministers have read gays out of church publicly, following supposedly "private" conferences.

From a pastoral viewpoint, the possibility of a reconsideration of church teaching is less immediately important than a revision of *practice* — specifically the cruel and unusual punishments doled out to gays by confessors, ministers, rabbis, boards of elders, synods, and preachers. Even a brief reexamination of the sources of the traditional teachings may well speed that process along.

SCRIPTURE AND TRADITION

A detailed analysis of scriptural and theological texts would go far beyond the intention of this book. Entire studies have been devoted to that, and while consensus is slowly emerging on certain issues, the questions remain complex and in many respects unconnected to the day-to-day situation of gay Christians.[2] One thing is abundantly clear, however. Later animosities toward homosexuality have consistently been read back into the Bible by translators ignorant both of ancient Hebrew customs and the early Christian situation. Such misinterpretations have then found use in justifying the condemnation and persecution of homosexual persons in a very non-biblical manner.

The central biblical tradition of opposition to homosexuality rests on very few texts, all but two of them highly controverted. Most of the oldest texts deal with male cult prostitutes (the *kedeshim*, e.g., Dt. 22:5; 1 Kings 14:24; 2 Kings 23:7; Hosea 4:14, etc.) and are not immediately relevant, although the context of idolatry should not be ignored for it figures in the background of almost every other reference. The more relevant Old Testament passages are Genesis 19:4-11 — the story of Sodom and Gomorrah, a parallel story in Judges 19:16-30, and two accounts from the Holiness Code of Leviticus 18:22 and 20:13.

The traditional association of Sodom and Gomorrah with homosexual vice has been subject to both ancient and recent criticism on scriptural grounds based on other biblical references which do not even allude to homosexuality as the cities' crime (e.g., Is. 1:9-10; Jer. 23:14; Lk, 10:12, Rev. 11:8, etc.). Of some twenty-two references, only two imply even the possibility of homosexual immorality (Ezek. 16:46f; 2 Peter 2:6). A third, Jude 7, a late Christian source strongly influenced by apocryphal Jewish writing, may allude to it. But the story of Lot and the men of Sodom did not receive a homosexual interpretation until the period of late Judaism, and then in Egypt in the writings of Philo. Such an interpretation did not enter Christian exegesis for two more centuries.

Scripture scholars admit that the Hebrew word *yadah* ("to know"), on which the entire issue hangs, is never used in relation to homosexual, i.e., anal intercourse, including the (only) indisputable references to homosexual practices in Lev. 18:22 and 20:13. Even as a euphemism for heterosexual intercourse, *yadah* is used only ten times in all of scripture. Its other 933 instances simply refer to direct, first-hand knowledge of something. Thus, the ironic play on "knowing" in Gen. 19 is at least ambiguous and most likely lacks any reference to homosexuality. Unless by "sodomizing" the Strangers, the men of Sodom intended "merely" to express political domination over them, among other absurdities, Lot's offer of his daughters as a sexual bribe would be stupid as well as evil.

But even if the Sodomites' immediate provocation had been attempted homosexual rape, that would not provide a basis for identifying the sin of Sodom with homosexuality rather than the violation of hospitality, which is the context for every further reference to Sodom in the Bible. Heterosexual rape was no less an abomination to the Jews, especially when it violated the law of hospitality, the obvious point of the parallel story of the Levite and his concubine in Judges 19 (Cf. also Dt. 22:25f.).

Rape is not at issue, however, in Leviticus 18:22 and 20:13, which appear in a section concerned with ritual purity and family integrity. These are the only clear references to homosexuality in the Old Testament, if not the whole Bible. But even here it is not certain that the "separateness" of Israel was not more important in the mind of the priestly writers than the specific malice of homosexuality. However that may be, the message is plain: "You shall not lie with a male as with a woman...." Significantly, only in Lev. 20:13 is the death penalty attached, although there is not a single case in the Bible of any execution for homosexual behavior.

The phrase "as with a woman" appears in both texts and should be considered carefully. Although unlikely among the un-philosophical Hebrews, (male) homosexuality could be taken here to represent a voluntary perversion of the natural sexual instinct. But it more likely signified the abasement of a male to female status, a degradation abhorrent throughout the Middle East. (In the ancient world and well into the modern era, forced submission to anal intercourse was routinely inflicted on defeated armies by their conquerors as a show of dominance.) If a free choice, especially by recourse to cult prostitutes, homosexual behavior acquired the malice of idolatry. In such a milieu, of course, the question of constitutional homosexuality could never arise at all.

In the New Testament, except for the questionable references in 2 Peter and Jude, there are only three references to possible homosexuality, all of them in the Pauline writings. Curiously, in Romans 1:26ff, where Paul is railing against idolatrous pagan worship, he does not use the term which appears in I Cor. 6:9 and I Tim. 1:9-10 (*arsenokoitai*), which probably means "male prostitute."[3] But the context in Romans is clearly one of cult prostitution, as was that of most Old Testament references. Involvement in such perversity, Paul insists, represents the tragic legacy of idolatry.

The terms *arsenokoitai* and *malachoi* which appear in

1 Corinthians and 1 Timothy among standard lists of sins might mean "homosexual males" rather than "male prostitutes," although it is significant that the words were apparently not taken in that sense either before or after St. Paul.[4] It is even more significant that neither these terms nor further references to male homosexuality (or prostitution) appear in the ten other such lists in the Pauline writings, the four lists in other writings, or in the gospels. But even if Paul actually meant "homosexual males," there is no more reason in these two passages than in Romans to suppose that the author had anything else in mind than indulgence in homosexual acts by heterosexual men, probably in the context of pagan rites. Paul could have had no knowledge of constitutional homosexuality. For him, as for his ancestors, homosexual behavior could only represent a deliberate perversion practiced on or by someone (constitutionally) heterosexual. (It is unclear whether the "unnatural" relations adopted by women (Rom. 1:26) were homosexual or heterosexual, although the latter is more likely, given Paul's use of antithesis. If so, there is no biblical reference whatsoever to female homosexuality, as in generally the case in law and religion.)

Overall, the general paucity of biblical references to homosexuality indicates that it was hardly a major concern for the ancient Jews, Jesus, Paul, or other Christian writers. It is important to bear in mind, further, that the Church has not employed even the few clear texts to condemn homosexual persons individually or as a whole. (In fact, those who use such texts to do so should consult St. Paul's immediately following prohibition in Rom. 2:1-11.) Rather, the meaning of the New testament sin lists is that no such immoral behavior befits members of the Kingdom of God.

Later polemics against sexual perversion of all kinds by the Greek and Latin Fathers are well known and were probably warranted. Sts. John Chrysostom and John Damascene would fulminate against the baths today as they did a millennium ago, and undoubtedly for the same reasons. The great medieval theologians were likewise concerned with homosexuality as a

perversion of heterosexual inclination as well as institution-
alized vice. This tradition has continued to the present,
generally following their lines of argumentation. However,
much of their case is debatable today on grounds similar to
those which call into question the scriptural and patristic
condemnations: an understandably inadequate grasp of
human physiological and psychological development as well as
scant information about animal behavior, upon which much of
their case rested. (An even deeper issue concerns how difficult
scripture and traditional theological texts are to be used in
contemporary moral teaching and pastoral practice.)

What concerns us more today is what Philo, Paul, John
Damascene, and Thomas Aquinas did not know: that true
homosexuality does not result from a willful decision to "give
up" heterosexuality, nor do most homosexual men and women
lead lives of wild sensuality and irresponsible lust. Psychologically speaking, constitutional homosexuality is a relatively
recent discovery. The distinction between "innate" and
"acquired" homosexuality was first seriously proposed in 1863,
and, although the notion of "congenital" homosexuality has
been abandoned, since the time of Freud scientific thought has
tended to accept constitutional homosexuality as a predominant,
irreversible orientation acquired through a long developmental
process beginning in early infancy, possibly even in the womb,
but one in which the individual exercises only minimal
direction.

In brief, constitutional homosexuality was not dealt with in
scripture, in traditional theology, nor even in recent Vatican
documents on sexual ethics and pastoral care, which in their
three "divisions" of transient, innate, and pathologically
constitutional homosexuality overlooked the largest class of all:
the healthy homosexual population. However, errors and
omissions concerning astronomy, biology, and paleontology
which were incorporated into Church teaching did not outdate
the message of salvation recorded in the Bible and preached by
the Church. Nor should the need to incorporate the findings of
psychologists and sociologists concerning homosexuality

occasion fear about compromising the essential morality of the Judeo-Christian heritage. For, as we shall see, Christian gays as a whole neither accept nor promote a double standard of morality.

CURRENT TEACHING

Present theological opinion on the status of homosexuality is varied. Some moralists maintain or imply that homosexuality and heterosexuality are on equal footing ethically and psychologically, being alternative forms of human sexuality. Proponents of the traditional position hold that homosexuality represents an intrinsic disorder and can in no wise fulfill the divinely appointed purposes of human sexuality. While carefully noting that as a condition, homosexuality is not a sinful state as such, traditionalists argue that any deliberate genital expression of that condition would be sinful.[5] At best, homosexual "unions" are a "lesser evil" than outright promiscuity or compulsive behavior, but nevertheless represent an objectively sinful situation and may not be approved of directly.[6]

My own opinion is that both approaches tend to miss the point. Given the complex and systematic nature of human sexuality, the psychological, physiological, and sociological complementarity of male and female persons means that heterosexuality obviously constitutes the common and therefore primary normative condition through which human persons can realize their sexual potential most completely. Further, heterosexual intercourse is the normal and (for the foreseeable future) *only* way in which the human race is propagated. Homosexuality obviously differs from this situation. But there are many manifest areas of complementarity among persons of the same (as well as the opposite) gender which are not based on sexual differences but on the commonness of human nature. Therefore, even apart from heterosexual attraction and reproduction, homosexuality is neither an alternative nor an abnormality in the sense of a pathological condition, which is clear from the clinical evidence of persistent and extensive health among homosexual men and women despite their "minority" status. Rather, homosexuality constitutes a *variation* within the normal range of human differences, gender differences among them. Moreover, it is a *natural* variation, not a sickness or a fault or a psychological, physiological, or sociological aberration, although any of these may accompany homosexuality in individual cases just as they do heterosexuality.

The fact of homosexuality may well arise because of some aspect of what Gabriel Marcel called "the brokenness of the world," an interpretation which can be neither proved nor disproved. Even if it is true, however, homosexuality cannot thereby be reckoned a "natural evil" alongside congenital defects and birth accidents. For homosexuality is not congenital, or a defect, or an accident, but an acquired difference in sexual orientation which is multi-causal and has many possible manifestations, as discussed in Chapter Two. Further, the behavioral difference between heterosexuality and homosexuality is a matter of degree of preference rather than a sharp divergence of kind, as all knowledgeable researchers affirm.

Asserting the moral superiority, inferiority, or equality of the varieties of human sexuality is therefore pointless. Just as some homosexual persons can be healthier in any number of ways than many heterosexual persons, and vice versa, many homosexual relationships are undoubtedly superior to many heterosexual marriages, and vice versa. However, in view of the commonly accepted values of human society and Christian culture, heterosexuality clearly remains the ideal condition for men and women, as theologians clearly sympathetic to the homosexual cause themselves admit.[7]

Nevertheless, even though a departure from the ideal "given" of the human condition, homosexuality persists as a constant factor in all human cultures. I believe that as such a "standard deviation" it too possesses a normative character, but one subordinate to and dependent upon heterosexuality. Further, it possesses a positive place and function in human experience. That is, it is part of God's "mysterious plan" for the wholeness and salvation of the human race — both in the lives of particular persons and in the history of the human race.

Homosexuality is not a disease to be eradicated or a fault to be forgiven, but an opportunity for men and women to grow and develop into mature, loving, and responsible human persons — whether gay or straight. From a Christian perspective, moreover, as a component of human experience as a whole, homosexuality has been taken up and redeemed by the incarnational transformation of human nature by the Word of God. Thus, in many respects homosexuality contributes a dimension to human life without which our history and destiny on this planet would be far poorer.

Even beyond that, I believe that for individual persons and for the race, homosexuality has a positive meaning of its own, aspects of which I shall discuss further in the following chapters. Fundamentally, I see it as the revelation of the possibility of friendship among men and women of both the same and the opposite sexes, one based less on biological differences or attractions than on psychological and sociological complementarity and spiritual attractiveness. As a redemptive dimension of human sexuality, therefore, homosexuality can help to heal the wounds inflicted on humanity by inter- and intra-sexual competitiveness. To borrow a phrase from Henri Nouwen, a gay person can be the "wounded healer" through whom the potentially fatal aggressiveness of our race can find its cure by being transformed into the co-operativeness of true friendship.

On Curing

It is still a current belief among many churchmen, as mentioned earlier, that homosexuality is a sickness which can and therefore should be cured or reversed. For instance, despite evidence that after adolescence there is only a small likelihood of "substantial change" in sexual orientation, plus resistance even to the thought of changing, because some reorientation of sexual preference is not *impossible*, one established and liberal moral theologian recommends that change-therapy should nevertheless be advised for gays "whenever possible." Even he admits that it will probably fail. In other words, gays should be advised to devote a considerable amount of time, emotional energy, and, not least of all, money to an almost certainly hopeless quest before resigning themselves to the fact that "nothing more can be done." Then they may be advised to adopt a celibate life-style, or, if that is deemed impossible, permitted to continue receiving the sacraments even if in a "gay marriage," which is considered a lesser evil than a life of casual promiscuity.

Despite the benevolent intention of its author, such advice seems peculiarly antiquated and even heartless, considering the sometimes permanent damage done to the self-esteem, hope, trust, and budget of docile gays by psychiatric change-artists and behavioral mechanics, as well as the statistically established improbability of any positive change to begin with.

Before a confessor or advisor and, indeed, a gay client entertain any scheme to change sexual orientation, thus tampering with the deepest wellsprings of human personality, they should possess nothing less than moral certitude that there is a high probability of success, given 1) the person's desire and ability (including the financial resources) to undergo many months if not years of therapy or analysis, 2) some evidence that there is sufficient heterosexual experience or at least interest to warrant such an endeavor, that is, that the person is not merely seeking to escape the difficulties and pain of being gay, and 3) the availability of an experienced therapist who will not violate the human dignity of his client and who is sufficiently skilled to be able to distinguish and deal with the client's non-sexual problems, which may not only be serious but need prior attention.

A further caution: an advisor's, confessor's, or parent's (or whoever's) animosity to homosexuality and anxiety to see gays "straighten out" are *never* sufficent reason to advise or demand change-therapy. The penitent's or client's needs, desires, conscience and capacities *must* come first, if not in the name of justice and compassion, at least in the name of professional competence. Many psychiatrists and therapists, following Hooker, Freedman, Tripp, Weinberg, Hoffman, and others, have objected professionally to therapists' exacting monetary and other sacrifices from gays merely to attempt the unlikely task of altering their sexual orientation. Several have publicly denied the possibility of changing the orientation of a constitutionally homosexual person without serious and perhaps lasting personality change. Some argue that so-called "successes" do not constitute change so much as temporary diversions or the lasting suppression of all sexual interest, the psychological equivalent of castration.

These dissidents from the long-standing presumption that homosexuality is an illness that can be reversed or cured are growing in numbers and influence in the world of psychology and psychiatry. Significantly, even Freud, who distinguished between neurotic and non-neurotic ("healthy") homosexuality, was pessimistic about efforts to redirect sexual preference — a step into the twentieth century that churchmen might well emulate.[8]

FAITH HEALING

For some time, a small but evidently increasing number of evangelical clergymen, not content to rant against gays or command them to seek a psychiatric cure, have themselves undertaken to heal them of their "plight," whether defined as sickness or sin. While an improvement over the stake and flames, such an approach is hardly less objectionable than (and not much different from) that of the gay-changing psychiatrists and aversion therapists.

While not ruling out a miraculous displacement of someone on the heterosexual-homosexual continuum (in either direction), I have my doubts about the state of homosexual Christians "healed" in prayer meetings and exorcisms. The virtual total failure to follow-up on these "cases," as well as the general lack of criteria for determining what constitutes a cure, raises serious questions about the truth of all such claims and also about the ethics of the effort itself. From direct observation, I am sure that the last state of the victim is often worse than the first, as in the case of a young man I met who professed to have been healed by a traveling evangelist and was "straight," yet continued compulsively to haunt the baths and "tea-rooms" for sex.

In other respects, however, religious healing for gays is not only desirable but, I think, possible; I know of many women and men who have benefitted from such a ministry. I am referring to a healing of memories, a reconciliation with parents and other family members, an alleviation of guilt and self-doubt, and an improvement in the quality of human relationships from one of resentment, exploitation, and possessiveness to one of effective compassion, service, and encouragement toward growth and freedom. For some gays, such healing in their lives may lead them to a celibate life-style, or perhaps to a life of commitment in fidelity and constancy with another person. It will not, I am confident, make a gay or lesbian straight — although, as with psychotherapy, pseudo-homosexual reactions may well be alleviated for disturbed heterosexual persons.

The real spiritual healing gays so often desperately need is the grace of self-acceptance and affirmation. Were faith healers to begin with an understanding of their potential for help in this area, their ministry of healing would take on a more truly humane and thereby a more Christian tone.

GAY MORALITY

Many gays seem caught up in the same trap that has ensnared not a few moral and pastoral theologians, one made more dangerous by its dual force: first, the elevation of sexual behavior to an all-important position in life, and, second, the consequential tendency to relate to oneself and others primarily as "sex objects" or merely objects — including members of the opposite sex, people of color, unattractive and older persons, and so forth. Such a sexualization of existence is as fraught with problems for gays as it has been for Christians in general. Sexual behavior becomes a field of excessively heightened moral consciousness, either so dominating morality as practically to become synonymous with it, especially with regard to sin and guilt, or eventually assuming practical independence from ordinary morality. Some gays (and straights) go so far in reaction as to reject the validity of any general sexual norms and values, denying the sinfulness of any sexual behavior short of rape and child-abuse.

Such a reactionary attitude is self-defeating. For although the realm of sexuality is one of the most sensitive, fundamental, and humane dimensions of life — it is only *one*. Thus it must include reference to a wider sphere of moral values, norms, and even etiquette that can often be subtle, perhaps delicately so, as well as profound. For the same reason, sexual morality itself cannot be taken as the over-riding paradigm for the rest of life's concerns, but must figure proportionately in an overall Christian ethic as *part* of life and the Christian attitude toward life. And as there is one Christ, one baptism, and one faith, there *is* a basic morality for all Christians, whether "Jew or Greek, slave or free, male or female" (Gal. 3:28; cf. Col. 3:11), and I would add, gay or straight. Sex is no exception to the inclusive foundation of the moral life — unselfish love for God and for our neighbor (cf. Mt. 22:34-40).

Gays themselves frequently insist that despite a difference in sexual preference, they are just like everyone else — a premise ably supported by a good deal of research. But this is also a *moral* premise. As moral agents, gay Christians must experience sexuality in harmony with rather than in contrast to the rest of common Christian beliefs about life, whether in respect to the spheres of social relations, work, spirituality, politics, or play.

Several gay correspondents were very definite about the integrity of Christian moral life, and almost all have flatly (if sometimes regretfully) rejected anything like a double standard for gays and straights. "I think homosexual loving experiences are different from straight loving experiences, especially those in marriage; but love and the obligation to loved ones, and obligations to all people, are still part of the same universe in which there are certain moral absolutes." One woman in her early thirties wrote: "I don't see how our moral responsibilities could be different. Maybe I just don't understand what you mean. (I do think it's harder to fulfill our moral obligations — on that I could write a book.)" Another stated, "Yes, I have the same moral responsibilities as my non-gay friends; I do think, though, that morality may have to be specially interpreted for gays — it's scary because there are few 'Christian' models. The only morality that I have considered is that I must respect other persons as children of God; I must not use them for selfish ends; and must allow them to grow — even as I, too, want to grow."

SEXUAL ETHICS

Such moral considerations have definite practical implications. However, few if any reliable guides to ethical conduct now exist for gays.[9] But the fundamental healthiness and moral maturity of many gay men and women will be manifest in their actual behavior. That behavior in turn will show, especially over the long haul, certain patterns which are consistent and recognizable as a kind of implicitly rule-governed attitude. The pragmatic principle at work here is found in almost all classical ethics: to discover what is ethically appropriate, discover what is characteristic of the decisions, behavior, and values of a truly good person.

In fact, people are generally aware of someone in their midst who "has it together" and thus functions as an ethical model, probably rather unobtrusively and unselfconsciously. In all likelihood, several men and women will emerge as a kind of "corporate model" of maturity and wisdom. These people will most likely not be those who strive to be imitated or who enjoy telling others what to do. For an ethically mature person is usually characterized by a wide-ranging tolerance of other people's behavior and a refusal to become upset or judgmental when others fail to live up to standards he or she spontaneously sets for him- or herself.[10]

As the lives of more healthy and creative gay men and women are examined in literature and film, ethical values and conduct will also become more apparent through the inevitable process of comparison and contrast. Novels such as *The Front Runner, Maurice, Rubyfruit Jungle*; biographies and autobiographies of persons such as Gertrude Stein, Tennessee Williams, Christopher Isherwood, Charles Laughton, John Reid's *The Best Little Boy in the World*, Howard Brown's *Familiar Faces, Hidden Lives*; and films the caliber of *Word is Out, The Naked Civil Servant*, and *A Special Day* — all have contributed to an emergent sense of gay values capable of undergirding an authentic ethic. Needless to say, many of these stories and accounts will conflict with each other, as values and interpretations often do. But a sincere effort to learn from such vicarious experience will help clarify one's own values. Every good work of art is a challenge to grow.

The fundamental issue of both moral and psychological gay maturity concerns the spiritual quality of a person's attitude toward others with respect to dignity, freedom, and ultimate integrity. Christian sexual responsibility is the capacity and desire to respond to another person as a uniquely valuable and therefore infinitely lovable Self in terms of bodily intimacy, psychological mutuality, and spiritual growth. Such responsibility could well be summed up in two words: reciprocal care. Something less may be far from depravity or even sinfulness, but it nevertheless falls below the level of what every human person deserves and desires: the best. At the opposite end of the scale is a one-sided, egoistic, other-denying gratification of physical and psychological urges which is aptly summed up as rape. Each human being is aiming at one or other of these goals in every exercise of sexual freedom — toward the fullness of life or toward the vacant anonymity of death. The ethical and religious challenge is, of course, to choose life. Whether we in fact do or not will often be revealed only in the consequences of our behavior. "You will know them by their fruit" (Matt. 7:20).

OBJECTIFICATION

The tendency of many gays to define themselves and others in primarily sexual-genital terms (a tendency strongly reinforced by the gay world) should not be divorced from the same tendency on the part of many straight persons, nor from the fact that churchmen have reinforced that tendency in general by overemphasizing sexuality, and that in primarily negative ways. The gay version, however, is doubly disadvantageous. First, gays want to be accepted as ordinary people, not sexual deviants; but if sex is only a part of life, however beautiful, important, and fundamental, a life largely or wholly centered on sex *is* a deviation. Secondly, such a fixation is severely restrictive. It overrates qualities associated with sexual attractiveness, such as youth, good looks, physique, clothes, and "style" to the detriment of equally or more important values such as basic honestly, depth of personality, integrity, spiritual maturity, and other life-interests in general.

It is also true, however, that much of the obvious sexual-fetishism of gay life is more a feature of social interaction and recreation — the visible part of the gay ghetto — than a personality trait of individuals. Most gays are invisible at work, school, and church — in fact, most are accepted as straight by their non-gay associates. It is in the gay ghetto that the invisibility is replaced by a heightened visibility, heightened in great measure as a reaction to the preceding 9 to 5 masquerade. Nevertheless, it is the after-dark world, where gays can be gay, that the frenetic mating rituals too often identified with homosexuality become a dominant thematic.

Sex is the motif of the ghetto — an inescapable, pervasive, almost demonic presence- to-mind that overshadows or at least shades every other aspect of experience. From a psychological viewpoint, such a situation is rightly called obsessive. In extreme cases, sexual obsession is a serious problem — whether for an individual or a society. In milder forms it seems to be common enough to have left its mark on a considerable portion of American culture. But whether or not we take it for granted, none of us is comfortable with the sexualization of life, nor even is the gay ghetto.

The virtually total sexualization of gay life affects individuals variously, but the major effect is one of "objectification" or depersonalization — the centering of attention on genital experience and even the genitals. The psychic fragmentation of personality involved in sexualizing experience produces both psychological and moral disintegration.

The first stage of sexual dis-integration is the tendency to relate to oneself or others primarily as sex-objects, even psychically isolating parts of the body from the whole. Interests, values, ideas, conversation, friends, and eventually the whole range of human experience are progressively focussed on the sexual element. The effects of such objectification have already been mentioned: a never-ending series of affairs, the prolonging of adolescence into middle age, a horror of aging, and few if any lasting relationships, especially on the sexual plane: as someone quipped, "in the ghetto, best friends don't screw."

A second phase of personal objectification is the progressive separation of love and sex. It is a mistake to *identify* love with sex, for many forms of love do not involve overt sexuality. Yet to divorce sex from love is to deprive both of their completion. From a Christian perspective, sex without love is a travesty of human dignity; a marriage without love may still be a legal contract, but it can hardly be called sacramental. And in the gay world, sex is plentiful, but lasting love often seems to be forever just beyond reach of many.

In the next chapter, I shall turn to some particular aspects of gay life in the context of spirituality. Here, I think it appropriate to conclude by recalling the presence of the Church institutionally within the gay ghetto, a harbinger, perhaps a catalyst, of a coming reconciliation between the "Church Catholic" and one of its largest estranged constituencies.

THE CHURCH IN THE GHETTO

The men and women gathered to study and implement the new rite of reconciliation described earlier were members of a local chapter of Dignity, an international Catholic organization of gays and concerned straights founded in 1969 in California. Dignity is committed to advancing the acceptance of gays in the church by promoting worship, spiritual development, education and constructive social action and recreation. There are over 5000 registered members in over one hundred chapters in the United States with affiliates in Canada, Australia, England, and Sweden. Still more thousands of men and women are associated with Dignity-sponsored activities such as liturgies and workshops. Over a thousand priests and religious men and women are involved in Dignity's work, some as chaplains, others as regular members.

A lay movement rather than an official church organization, for almost two decades Dignity was quietly welcomed in some dioceses, while merely tolerated or even banned in others. Following the publication of Cardinal Ratzinger's "Letter on the Pastoral Care of Homosexual Persons" at Halloween, 1986, however, the Roman Curia began pressuring American bishops to deny Dignity the use of church facilities. A handful of United States and Canadian bishops quickly fell into line. Significantly, most have not yet found it necessary to disown Dignity, which, as a national organization, expressed support of Pope John Paul II on his visit to the United States in the autumn on 1987, while continuing to dissent from some curial positions.

Never intended to be a separatist movement, Dignity provides an opportunity for fellowship and worship for Christian men and women who have been rejected by or simply feel unwelcome among their straight brothers and sisters. As a ministry to the "unwanted," it has brought back thousands of

Catholics to the Church and enhanced the religious commitment of many more. The following testimony of a man of fifty is not unlike that of many other gays, most of whom prefer to remain Catholic rather than break away: "I returned to the Church after a long absence through my association with Dignity. I felt the Church was giving me an opportunity to serve God through her as the person I really am." Another commented, "I can hardly conceive of being accepted in a straight parish, unless the world changes drastically. I think gay people will always be, to a great extent, outsiders, and they will find their most meaningful and rewarding experiences in communities like ours." A young woman added, "The beautiful part about *this* gay community is that it is a *real* community. There is a bond, a connectedness, a relatedness, a group feeling, a personal feeling."

Courage, a more traditionally Catholic organization, which requires an express commitment to sexual abstinence of its members, was founded in 1980 by Fr. John Harvey and others at the behest of Cardinal Terence Cooke. About eight groups now exist in the United States and Canada. Similar movements, such as Exodus International, Homosexuals Anonymous, Metanoia Ministries, Outpost, and Regeneration exist in conservative Protestant denominations.[11]

Other, less stringent organizations or movements for acceptance exist within Christian and Jewish denominations. In 1968 the Metropolitan Community Church was founded by Rev. Troy Perry as a distinct congregation. Protestant and evangelical, MCC has churches throughout the world and claims over 20,000 members. Integrity, an Episcopal outreach program, works primarily within the main body of the church rather than sponsoring separate worship services. Like Dignity, Integrity sponsors national conventions which feature well-known speakers and draw hundreds of participants. Effective gay caucuses exist in Lutheran, Presbyterian, and Methodist denominations as well as the Orthodox Church. The United Churches of Christ have initiated programs, as have the Society of Friends, several pentecostal churches, and

Mormon groups. Jewish congregations which include admitted gays exist in larger metropolitan areas. Needless to say, the range of views on the origin, morality, "curability," and spirituality of homosexuality vary enormously.[12]

Gays exist, of course, within the institutional church as well as in dissident satellites. Despite the (fallacious) opinion that, as one venerable religious writer recently informed gays, "You are barred from the priesthood... and... must be weeded out of religious orders," a rather conservative estimate of the number of homosexual men and women in the Catholic priesthood and religious life, according to an informal census of priests and religious at a recent workshop, falls around thirty percent. (The figure given by the *National Catholic Reporter* in a series of recent articles estimates the percentage to be even higher.[13]) A significant number of gays exercise their ministry as Protestant clergy and in the rabbinate as well. But whatever the actual percentage gay and lesbian clergy may represent, I am sure that their percentage in the Kingdom of Heaven will be far greater yet.

NOTES

1. I am indebted here to the unpublished research of Dr. John Boswell of Yale University. Cf. also Arno Karlen, op. cit. pp. 86ff.
2. Among other important discussions are those in the works by Bailey, Boswell, Macourt, McNeill, Nugent, Scanzoni and Mollencott listed in the Resources for Further Study below, pp. 181ff.
3. In his essay "Lexicography and St. Paul," Dr. John Boswell argues that this term, found only in these places, does not in fact have the meaning later associated with it. Significantly, St. Paul did not use any of the ordinary Greek terms for homosexuality current in his time, which has raised the question for some exegetes whether he was referring to homosexuality at all. Cf. *Christianity, Social Tolerance, and Homosexuality*, op. cit., pp. 335-53.
4. See Boswell, op. cit., pp. 345-53, and the discussion by Rictor Norton and James Martin in Macourt, ed. cit., pp. 39-60.
5. "Although the particular inclination of the homosexual person is not a sin, it is a more or less strong tendency ordered toward an intrinsic moral evil; and thus the inclination itself must be seen as an objective disorder." "Letter to the Bishops of the Catholic Church on the Pastoral Care of Homosexual Persons," Rome: Sacred Congregation for the Doctrine of the Faith, Oct. 1, 1986, p. 4. Cf. the "Declaration on Sexual Ethics," Dec. 29, 1975. Both are available through

the Publications Office of the United States Catholic Conference, Washington, D.C. Counseling positions espousing this viewpoint can be found in John F. Harvey, O.S.F.S., *The Homosexual Person: New Thinking in Pastoral Care*, San Francisco: Ignatius Press, 1987, and John R. Cavanaugh, M.D., *Counseling the Homosexual*, Huntington, Indiana: Our Sunday Visitor Press, 1977.

6. A modification of this principle is expressed in the pastoral letter of the Bishops of England and Wales, op. cit., p. 8: "There has been an attempt to establish parity between a normal marriage and the on-going homosexual relationship. This is a false and unacceptable analogy. The pastor may distinguish between irresponsible, indiscriminate sexual activity and the permanent association between two homosexual persons, who feel incapable of enduring a solitary life devoid of sexual expression. This distinction may be borne in mind when offering pastoral advice and establishing the degree of responsibility, but the pastor will not be providing true and helpful advice if he gives the impression that the 'homosexual marriage' is objectively moral."

7. Cf. John McNeill, *The Church and the Homosexual*, p. 160. But see also p. 122f.

8. A hopeful sign was given by the Bishops of England and Wales in their pastoral letter of 1979, which stated, "In the case of true homosexuals or 'inverts', professional therapy may be helpful to assist them in accepting their condition positively, but therapy should never be suggested in a way that raises false expectations of a reverse or modification of the homosexual condition" (p. 12).

9. A growing ethical awareness can be found in many sources, including McNeill, op. cit., pp. 129-48; see the works listed in the Resources for Further Study by Pittenger, Oberholzer, Weltge; and popular works such as Don Clark's *Loving Someone Gay*, Millbrae, California; Celestial Arts, 1977 and 1987 (revised ed.).

10. In this respect see the writings of Lawrence Kohlberg, especially "Moral Stages and Moral Development," in Thomas Lickona, ed., *Moral Development and Behavior*, (New York: Holt, Rinehart and Winston, 1976), and especially James Fowler's *Stages of Faith: The Psychology of Human Development and the Quest for Meaning*, San Francisco: Harper and Row, 1981.

11. Many of these groups reflect a fundamentalistic approach to homosexuality and aim at "curing" or reorienting homosexual persons towards heterosexuality with a view to marriage. For a largely sympathetic discussion of these groups and their objectives, see John Harvey, *The Homosexual Person*, op. cit., pp. 120-58.

12. A partial list of national religious organizations can be found in the Resources for Further Study below, p. 181ff.

13. Cf. *National Catholic Reporter*, "Homosexuality in the Priesthood Said to Run High," by Jason Berry, 23, 18 (27 Feb. 1987): 1, 16-20. See also Richard McBrien, "Homosexuality and the Priesthood," *Commonweal* 114, 12 (19 June 1987): 380-83.

CHAPTER SEVEN

Gay Spirituality

AS the gay constituency of the Christian community has grown more visible, the need to articulate an explicitly gay spirituality has also become more evident. To many gay Christians, this may seem redundant, for they have already satisfactorily integrated their sexuality into their Christian life. For other Christians, a gay spirituality represents an impossibility, either because homosexuality is considered an intrinsic disorder, something to be cured or at least to conceal, or, conversely, because it is considered an area of life (like sexuality in general) divorced from spiritual concern.

Segregating sexuality from spirituality either by suppression or by fission is injurious, however, both to the individual whose life is thus fragmented and to the church itself, which is impoverished by being forced to ignore an important aspect of human experience. If a gay spirituality is possible, it is necessary.

Further, a gay spirituality cannot be redundant, for explicitly or implicitly "straight" spiritualities fail gay men and women precisely where the difference becomes crucial. Despite large areas of mutual concern and actual congruence, gay and straight experience are simply not identical. To the extent that gay experience is distinctive, a gay spirituality is warranted.[1]

GAY SPIRIT

Implicit in the word "gay" is a fundamental affirmation of the positive meaning and moral value of homosexuality as an integral part of personality structure and functioning, and an ineradicable component of the human condition itself. To be a gay Christian means to experience being gay as an expression of God's loving plan for oneself as part of the whole human family. This is to say that homosexuality has been assumed with every other human situation by the redemptive power of God's Word, who in the person of Jesus Christ expressed the concrete fullness of human nature — in its fallenness as well as its fundamental goodness, else the saving passion and glorification of Christ would not possess a truly universal power and dominion.

In terms of spirituality, therefore, the quest and attainment of wholeness includes the integration of human sexuality — both homosexual and heterosexual — as an important but partial factor within personality structure and actual experience. Moreover, to the extent that positive gay sensibilities, attitudes, values, life-style, and behavior find expression within Christian life as a whole, there the foundations of a gay spirituality are already present.

INTEGRATION; TOWARDS A CONTEMPORARY SPIRITUALITY

"Spirituality" is a double-barreled word. Taken as the conscious effort by which people organize and guide their lives in terms of religious values and principles, spirituality has a particular, even unique, dimension. In this respect, it is appropriate to refer to spiritualities rather than to spirituality. However, human life is also always social, religious life included. Individual spiritualities are largely derived from community experience, the surrounding culture, and ultimately from the whole Church as the sacrament of humanity.

Essentially, spirituality refers to the fundamental openness of human nature to transcendent experience, that is, an encounter with others which takes us beyond or "out" of ourselves. Because of the dynamic, temporal character of human existence, spirituality also refers to the process of realizing that capacity for transcendence by actual encounters of many kinds. Each such experience involves some dimension of the world beyond us which is raised to conscious awareness. Organized into the pattern of a whole way of life, therefore, every spiritual lifeway or "method" (the word comes the Greek, and means something like "following the road") always has an intrinsic social dimension.

Developing a spirituality is not so much a science as an art, the art of living. It respects and cultivates the bodily aspects of experience, including the sexual dimension. The mental discipline of meditation enjoys equal importance, but builds upon the spirituality of the body. Similarly, religious and aesthetic aspects of life such as the appreciation of beauty and the desire for goodness, the quest for justice, reverence for life, humor, playfulness, and especially friendship all find place in a truly integrative spirituality. As a process, moreover, each person's spirituality will be organized according to priorities which each woman or man assigns to the values represented by these characteristics. It will be expressed more in story, symbol, and action than in reflexive awareness. For symbols and myth, like gestures, convey what concepts and measurements cannot comprehend.

From a Christian perspective, such a personal spirituality means an individualized style of living in which body, mind, and spirit are consciously integrated in terms of a freely chosen system of beliefs and values centered on God's self-communication in Jesus Christ. Every Christian spirituality is thus developed by a continual integration of self, nature, and society into the whole Christ, and finds primary expression through worship, prayer, and service. This is no less true of a gay spirituality than any other. And although every variety of Christian spirituality is in its most concrete manifestation largely unique and therefore ineffable, certain characteristics will be commonly shared by all. The following represent a few of them.

First of all, every Christian spirituality will be *God-centered*, finding the Holy Spirit present in scripture, sacramental celebration, and in the world itself as the medium of creative

Love. And thus it will be *prayerful*, directly responding to God in praise, thanksgiving, and petition. But it will also be *social*, rooted and expressed in human communities of love and service, and attentive to God's presence in other persons. It will, likewise, be *natural*, attuned to God's active presence in and care for all creation. It will be no less *timely* — grounded historically in the saving events by which God continues to fashion a people. It will to that extent also be *ecclesial*, aware of the commonality of salvation realized here and now in the institutional and spontaneous aspects of the Church's corporate life and mission. Above all, it will be *Christological*, finding in Jesus Christ both model and mediator between God and human persons, "the human face of God," to borrow William Ernest Hocking's phrase. And because of that, it will be *compassionate*, expressing a passionate concern especially for the poor, oppressed, and suffering in works of peace, friendship, and justice.

THE SPIRITUAL DIALECTIC

Spirituality is above all else an integrative art, or, more accurately, a *re*-integrative one. We begin life as infants — well-integrated but hardly even conscious and certainly unable to survive independently. We mature and slowly gain control of our powers, but by dint of the world' brokenness, we arrive at self-conscious maturity more or less dis-integrated physically, psychologically, and spiritually. All of us, whether gay or straight, often need healing before we can grow further. Thus, there is a *therapeutic* as well as a *developmental* aspect to spirituality. Re-integration remedies our deficiencies and guides us along the way to fuller health — bodily, mental, and social. Spirituality guides this integrating process by providing a model and a method, both organically related to a coherent set of values.

The model and the goal of the process is the *whole* person, ultimately Christ himself, the full Christ — head and members.

Thus, the healing work of spirituality may be largely implicit in the social transactions between the individual person and the concerned community. In such cases, reintegration proceeds more or less unconsciously. But this therapeutic function may be facilitated and even abbreviated (or, better, condensed) by making it consciously explicit through spiritual counseling and direction.

Through the centuries, the dialectic of integration, disintegration, and re-integration has been given various designations. In Christian antiquity it was simply called the mystical life, later "the three ages" of the interior or spiritual life — that of beginners, the "proficient" or learners, and the "perfect" or fully mature (cf. 1 John 2: 12-15.). It was also described in terms of the "purgative," "illuminative," and "unitive" ways or stages of spiritual development, a functional characterization made most famous by St. John of the Cross. Fundamentally, the "three ways" refer to the spiritual process of purification, enlightenment, and integration by which the human person attains to integration and closer union with God.

While positive in meaning and function, in later centuries these stages were interspersed between "negative" transitional stages, the "dark nights" of the senses and the soul, as they were poetically described by St. John of the Cross. A modern writer, Dr. John Lilly, refers to the process as one beginning with "orthonoia" (conventional life), passing through "paranoia" (breakdown), and ending with "metanoia," or conversion to full human maturity.[2]

It is especially important to recognize with respect to gay spirituality that there are social factors at work in all three stages of the spiritual dialectic, whatever we call them. Part of the process that every human being has to undergo in order to become fully healthy includes the identification of and detachment from the socially conditioned values, concepts, attitudes, and behavioral patterns which, beginning as children, we adopt uncritically in the course of socialization itself. These social factors are not only a mixture of helpful and hurtful elements, they are powerfully compelling, the more so to the extent that they continue to function unconsciously. This process repeats itself whenever someone becomes a member of a sub-cultural community, the gay world being no exception.

No doubt, if young adults did not spontaneously come to the often painful recognition of the social construction of reality and the need for disengagement in order to become morally and conceptually autonomous or "self-actualizing," it would be necessary to induce such a detachment in order to promote full human maturity. For only when a person has acquired at least a minimal degree of social independence can she or he freely choose to adopt from among the goals, values, ideas, attitudes, and patterns of behavior available in a society those which can constitute a personally meaningful life-style. Thus, all detachment is for the sake of re-attachment.[3] This is doubly true for gay men and women, who often live in two social worlds simultaneously.

For social deconditioning may occur spontaneously but also without the supportive structures of an explicit spirituality to provide both the framework and control by which the process can be systematically advanced. That is, detachment can occur prematurely or without awareness of the possibility of re-attachment; disintegration can ensue without the hope of re-integration. A serious fragmentation of personality may result. Thus, many schizophrenics are probably undeveloped or aborted mystics, just as many tramps, thieves, and other social misfits could be considered arrested saints.[4] This bears importantly on the situation of gay persons who, frequently by coming out, have suddenly uncovered the mechanics of social determinism in their own lives and had to face the limits of their previous social conditioning. To that extent they are free of them. But they may not have access to an alternative integrating framework and control system except that of the gay world itself, which is fraught with its own social determinants. Perhaps the only genuine alternative to becoming either "paranoid" or a creature of the ghetto is to develop an explicit and authentic spirituality.

SOCIAL DIMENSIONS OF SPIRITUALITY

From a natural viewpoint (that is, apart from considerations of grace), it is the social basis of spirituality, its anchorage in the deepest values and highest aspirations of the human species, that provides through the concrete experience of men and women everywhere and at all times a relatively trans-cultural structure which can safely undergird the program of social disengagement. Spiritual development thus stabilizes the dialectic of disintegration and reintegration by supplying a fundamental continuity of experience. It also makes more basic criteria of evaluation available and exposes a wider range of options out of which a deeper and more personal value system can be constructed. Finally, it offers the concrete opportunity and resources for a controlled withdrawal from and return to society. This it does by functioning as a way of life in a supportive community funded by years, perhaps centuries, of collective experience, supplying motivation in the form of encouragement and goals, and providing guidance or direction by the ministry of skilled helpers. If the group embodying these elements concretely has a history of any scope, there will also be concrete models or examples to imitate or surpass in the form of heroes or saints. This will be as true of the gay world as of any cultural system.

The culmination of the dialectic of spiritual development occurs when a more or less continuous stage of personal unification is retained, although the persistent brokenness of the world guarantees only approximate success in this achievement. Such unification is not attained by attending to one's own progress, moreover, but by a progressively closer identification with the transpersonal Other. Full spiritual development can only be realized in social experience, because we are social beings both by nature and by grace. The Unitive Way is thus marked by an ever-growing awareness of oneness with God and also of oneness with our brothers and sisters "in the Lord."

This unity is first and primarily realized in the mutual dialogue and self-giving of true worship. It is secondarily but equivalently found in the re-entry into the world of other persons, nature, and society, wherein the God of mystical awareness also works and waits. The sign of true sanctity (which literally means wholeness or integrity) is charity, what the New Testament calls *agape* — a love expressed tirelessly in service and care. But connected with this divine love is an equally powerful thirst for justice and the spread of justice in all human relationships. The mystic, for so we may name the one who has begun the quest for the ultimate integrity of human life, is also the prophet.

But the achievement, or rather, the inauguration of final integrity is not the simple effect of a human process of spiritual development. It comes at last as a gift for which we can only make ourselves ready by ridding our lives of obstacles and positively surrendering our efforts to reach God. And the communication of God in love to a heart made receptive by abandoning its own plans for fulfillment is rightly called *grace* — the freely given and shared life of God itself.

TOWARDS A GAY SPIRITUALITY

In light of this sketch of the foundations of Christian spirituality, a gay spirituality will be distinguished by reference to the specific characteristics of healthy gay experience, both individual and social. First of all it will be *gay*. The transcendent dimension of experience must be found in context of the particular life-situations of gay persons. Likewise, the integration of body, mind, and spirit will involve the specific difficulties, opportunities, and hopes of gay men and women. The social aspects of worship, friendship, and justice will also reflect the exigencies of gay life and society, as well as relations with straight men and women, and facets of social prospects and oppression.

To begin with, gay spirituality, like any other, is always a social process. As observed earlier, the elements of every spirituality are derived from other s — and in particular from the immediate environment with its specific attitudes, values, and patterns of behavior. A gay spirituality, then, will reflect t he social structure and dynamics of the gay world as a social subsystem. It, too, will require raising to greater consciousness the positive and negative fact ors latent in gay experience, assessing them in order to incorporate what is constructive for each individual and the community. An authentic gay spirituality will thus also function as a critique of the gay world within the context of the wider social milieu.

Of particular importance here is the "deautomatizing" power in being gay, which endows the gay man or woman with the ability to see with different eyes, that is, to disengage themselves from the value-systems uncritically accepted in society at large. This can be frightening and even dis-integrative. It can also be liberating, both for gays and ultimately for straight people. Specifically, it gives gay men and women the power to risk decisions about life which straight men and women do not even consider because of their greater stake in the dominant social system.

POSITIVELY DETACHED

Although the vast majority of gay men and women are "out" only in a limited sense, an authentic gay spirituality must recognize that acceptance, association, and action represent the cutting edge of a fundamentally healthy gay identity, individu-ally and collectively. In a society rendered increasingly homogeneous and colorless by mass communication, transporta-tion, commerce, education, and entertainment, being a member of a subculture possesses distinct advantages for anyone seeking a meaningful niche in the social world. For a gay man or woman, a sense of commonality, of having a special character which, although not freely chosen, nevertheless relates them to other gays throughout the world and offers a distinctive place and role. It isn't a wholly comfortable niche — but it does serve to differentiate them from the mass society, if somewhat negatively.

This sub-cultural identification process should not be underestimated as a factor in a person's decision to come out — or, rather, to *stay* out. If merely a compensation for failing to achieve a more ordinary social identity, it can have an inhibiting effect on personality development. But it can also open up possibilities for growth and personality development, apart from any question of sexual behavior. In either case, as an encompassing way of life, the social experience of gay men and women bears significantly on their spirituality.

Thus, the more or less traditional opinion of spiritual writers that homosexual men and women should avoid all situations, persons, or references connected with homosexuality — in other words, to stay in or go *back* to the "closet" — has become untenable today. For by encouraging suppression and denial in the case of an inclination as primal and powerful as sexuality, such advice will probably produce not mental peace but greater distress, anxiety, and explosive episodes of compulsive sexual indulgence. "Being out" is a far more positive route with regard to mental health, and true mental health and spirituality can never be opposed.

Flight from the gay world is no more "spiritual" than flight from the world in general. On the other hand, uncritically identifying yourself with the whole gamut of experiences, institutions, and life-styles in the gay world is just as much a capitulation of moral discernment and autonomy as is the sad and mindless conformity still so characteristic of our life in society. It is even more foolish to place yourself in a situation in which a real moral failure is practically inevitable. The favorite adage of Socrates (and St. Bernard) is still applicable: "Know yourself." Then act accordingly.

In brief, spiritually healthy gay Christians of the future will more likely than not be known — at least selectively — to be gay, and most will certainly not masquerade as straight. This will be as true for sisters, priests, and brothers as it is for laypersons. For a gay man or woman to be called to a life of dedication to God in the service of God's people does not differ from the vocation of straight men and women. For a gay person, however, such a life will be more difficult in some respects, not because of temptations, but because of the extreme "homophobia" found in seminaries, convents, novitiates, and the institutional church as such.

The process of "coming out" itself has many of the characteristics of religious conversion, as noted earlier. With regard to personality integration, it can have the same function in a gay spirituality. But in this respect, as in the other, entrusting yourself to God by saying "yes" is not the climax. It is only the prologue. The exuberance wears off, and the let-down in either case can be severe as, perhaps for the first time, the convert begins to face the responsibilities and day-to-day grind of following through. It is at this point that a realistic and workable spirituality is most necessary.

TRANSCENDENCE

As a radical capacity for transcendent experience, gay spirituality is essentially no different from that of anyone else. However, societal pressures on gays are generally greater, and their proportionate awareness of the need for a deeper source of personal security and worth does, I think, affect their readiness to deal with the transcendent dimension of human experience in a positive way.

Years ago, the great depth-psychologist Carl Jung expressed this well when writing about male homosexuality in "The Mother-Son Complex" (I believe his remarks pertain no less to lesbians): "Often he is endowed with a wealth of religious feelings, which help him bring the *ecclesia spiritualis* into reality, and a spiritual receptivity which makes him responsive to revelation."[5]

Whatever Jung meant by the *ecclesia spiritualis*, it is evident that many gay men and women are remarkably sensitive to religion — both positively and negatively. Few gays I have met are indifferent about it or the Church, especially concerning the role that the latter has played in oppression and discrimination

— and still does. On a deeper level, as a minority group gays are perhaps acutely aware of the pretentiousness and brokenness of the social world. This, I think, also accounts for their evident openness to signals of transcendence from beyond the wreckage.

Here, too, I find a clue to the almost characteristic "fixing" enthusiasm which is virtually a gay stereotype. With what I can describe only as a kind of yearning for grace and beauty, gays seem to have a penchant for rehabilitating old houses, preserving architecture, restoring antiques, conserving park areas, playgrounds, and old traditions of all kinds. Whole sections of urban blight have been renovated largely by gay effort and example. Similarly, many gays can be found in the healing and service professions as doctors, dentists, nurses, paramedical personnel, orderlies, social workers, therapists, counselors, clergy, lay ministers, teachers, and more. It is as if both the human and aesthetic wreckage of society appeal in a special way to the sensitivities of those who have also suffered rejection — and who thus richly fulfill Henri Nouwen's description of the "wounded healer."

Gays are also susceptible to sentimentalism and aestheticism, just as some are to insensitivity and even vandalism. Given the bright side, the shadow should be expected to show the same contours. But overall, and for a variety of reasons, the capacity for transcendence, for ecstatic experience, seems well-developed among most gays. A hint of this appears in anthropological and archaeological studies of religion, especially of shamanism. Mircea Eliade and other researchers point out that among many pristine cultures, homosexuality was even taken to be a sign of divine election.[6]

BODY, MIND, AND SPIRIT

The corporal aspects of spirituality have always lurked in the background of classical treatments. Generally the body was treated as an enemy to be purged, mortified, punished, and generally scorned. This persistent Manichaeism still infects a large part of contemporary spirituality, but the tide is at last turning.

The body is far more than a container for the soul. It is the soul, the self, made manifest — the visible sacrament of the human spirit. Our treatment of the body, correspondingly, is a metaphor or index of our attitude toward ourselves. Today especially, when a negative self-image seems to be the native endowment of the race, it is vitally important to begin a spiritual program therapeutically — by "unlearning" abuse of the body and learning how to befriend and "tune" it properly.

This is true in general in our society. But because of the traditionally severe and negative attitude of society and the church toward homosexuality, it is even more urgent for a gay spirituality to reintegrate the self corporally. Negatively, this means neither pampering yourself, substituting cosmetic art for true care, nor abusing yourself physically, nor permitting yourself to be abused. Positively, all the dimensions of bodily personality need to be understood, appreciated, and cultivated. This entails not only developing some effective body-consciousness, but attending to the "asceticism" of proper diet, exercise, rest, eye care, skin and hair care, dental hygiene, and the maintenance of the various internal systems — including the bodily aspects of sexuality.

To abuse, neglect, or permit abuse of the body is symptomatic of psychological and spiritual problems. Caring for yourself, conversely, touches on some sensitive areas of our society in general — alcohol consumption, other drug abuse, including "ordinary" drugs such as caffeine, nicotine, and the various barbiturates and other ingredients of sleeping pills, stimulants, and the endless variety of so-called "recreational" drugs — marijuana, cocaine, "crack," and so forth. Such exotic forms of chemical ecstasy are common enough in the gay world. But the body can tolerate only a limited amount of physical abuse, no matter how "enjoyable," before lasting damage results — including damage to the mind and, proportionately, to the spirit. Acquainting yourself beforehand with the effects even of mild drugs such as marijuana, amyl and butyl nitrate, and especially the more dangerous kinds — amphetamines, cocaine, opium, and heroin — may prevent serious problems later on.[7]

Affirmative action with respect to the physical dimension of our existence is the bedrock of any contemporary spirituality. Regular exercise and periodic medical checkups are no less beneficial to gays than to straight people and with regard to AIDS and other venereal diseases, even more so. Similarly, weight-watching, body-building, some forms of aerobic exercise, Tai-chi, and dance, like running and other ordinary athletics, can be excellent forms of ascetical discipline. In the area of physical fitness, fortunately, gays seem to have anticipated the "health craze" of the 'eighties among the U.S. population as a whole.

SPIRITUALITY AS MINDFULNESS

Spiritually, the ancient Greek ideal of a healthy mind in a healthy body has not been superseded by the industrial revolution and the atomic age. Because of mechanization and industrialization, in fact, we are probably less likely than our Attic ancestors to preserve either physical or mental health despite our spectacular triumphs over certain diseases. "Getting your head together" pretty well sums up the challenge, both for gay and straight people. But in many respects, the passage from orthonoia to paranoia is shorter for gays, given the hostile emotional climate in which they are forced to live. The clear message to every gay man and lesbian at one time or another, even all the time, is simply that "You are definitely not OK." But the journey to metanoia, "new-mindedness" or, even better, "Christ-mindedness," is far from impossible for gays even in the midst of continual accusations of mental or moral pathology. In many ways, considering the enormous pressure constantly weighing down on them, gays may become mentally healthier than their straight counterparts, as noted earlier.[8]

With regard to gay spirituality, mental integrity consists in right thinking and right attitudes about yourself, the world at large, and all those "special persons" in your life. As a condition for mental freedom, disengagement from ordinary social concepts and patterns of behavior may come easier for gays, as discussed earlier. Disciplined thinking, however, like thinking for yourself, is no one's birthright. Merely substituting one set of social concepts for another is no solution to the problem of mental dis-integration. We all have to relearn how to think rightly and well by first unlearning some poor thinking.

In spirituality, the art of such "mindfulness" has traditionally been called *meditation*. Fundamentally, it is the ability to arrest conceptual thinking and to cultivate awareness — experiencing the simple fact of Be-ing. As a mental discipline, meditation recreates the mind just as exercise and rest refresh the body. It simplifies consciousness by widening its focus and thus helps restore psychological balance and integrity. From a religious perspective, the art of meditation in its many varieties has but one goal: to rid the mind-field of distracting images and concepts and thus to "tune" it to the pervading presence of God, the unobjectifiable Ground of all our experience. Eventually, the voluntary stillness of meditative concentration gives way to an effortless contemplative "gaze," a still deeper form of non-analytic, pre-reflexive awareness. With this, the human spirit completes its preparation and must await the free gift of God's presence, revealed now not as the dimly perceived Ground of our experience, but as the manifest awareness of a Friend and Companion alongside us.[9]

From a gay viewpoint, perhaps the most salient feature in the process of meditation is its ability to break down habitual modes of thinking and acting, that is, its capacity for "deautomatization" or dishabituation. Having shaken loose the pervasive control which socially determined concepts exercise over thought and action by becoming still and momentarily suppressing conceptual thinking itself, it becomes possible to develop independent habits of thought and behavior by simply attending and responding to what truly Is. No one can ever break absolutely free from every constraint of the social patterns of knowledge and value, however. Human freedom is always relative. But breaking loose from an uncritical and therefore absolute dependence on the dominant social matrix is nevertheless real freedom, however relative — and no less dizzying for that.

Once spirituality is understood as the attempt consciously to integrate the various components of experience into a life-style centered on certain fundamental and freely chosen values, it is not difficult to see that sexual identification and social roles must play an important part in spiritual development. Ignoring or repressing them not only fragments the spiritual life, but permits sexuality to dominate it unconsciously. By contrast, a healthy spirituality will incorporate masculinity and femininity, generativity, and support. Further, sexuality will be recognized as an essential interpersonal dimension of life, not a matter of private preoccupation.[10]

Positively integrating sexual identity and role, including the dimension of orientation or emotional preference, presents particular challenges and opportunities for a gay man or woman. From their perspective, socially conditioned models of identity and role are discovered not only to be inapplicable in most respects, but also to be highly relative. Even the stereotypes of masculinity and femininity more or less unconsciously — if classically — imported into gay life-styles, such as "butch and nelly," or "dyke and femme" characteristics, served mainly to point out the artificiality of enforced poses. Today, the resistance of many gays unwilling to be superficially categorized has led to a greater exercise of creativity and responsibility in constructing styles of life satisfying to individuals on their own terms. Conversely, by sharply separating maleness and femaleness from cultural conceptions of masculinity and femininity, gay life-styles and even poses have had a liberating effect on straight society itself. Total femininity is as much a chimera as is male superiority, white supremacy, or "Western civilization" itself.

In a word, resisting the force of social systems bent on imposing roles on supposedly malleable individuals becomes a necessary, if negative, preliminary for developing a positive spirituality. Conversely, successfully integrating various personal competencies and exploring interesting role possibilities can develop into a whole program of self-liberation and spiritual development.

Spirit and Value

The realm of spirit concerns aspects of experience which are not easily analyzed — truth, freedom, happiness, beauty, reverence, humor, peace, and the awareness of supreme worth, goodness, and right. Among the greatest I would name the intellectual love of God, the commonwealth of human friendship, and the sense of cosmic wonder. However we envision them, all spirituality basically concerns *values* — what we esteem in things, persons, events, and life itself. But not in the abstract or as static attributes. Rather, spiritual values are always concrete, alive, and above all, active. Any spirituality which does not lead to active involvement in human affairs is radically un-Christian.

Three fundamental values can serve to exemplify the rest — justice, friendship, and worship, which summarize and virtually encompass all that is most worthwhile in human experience. Thus, as we near the conclusion of this sketch, we return to our original theme.

Worshiping

Worship represents the explicit acknowledgment of God in which the human spirit replies "Thou" to the divine self-communication in all the graced moments of life. As a moment in a dialogue, worship has an aspect of responsibility about it which suggests a form of justice. For worship recognizes and ratifies the right relationship, the *bond* between creatures and their Creator. Worship is also a form of friendship, for it also binds human persons together in corporate forms of prayerful celebration. Like human justice, our active expressions of praise, gratitude, reparation, and petition are moved from within by love. Worship is the vertical dimension of loving service in the human world.

In the gay part of that world, worship is not a manifestly predominant factor — but a movement toward God is nevertheless clearly present in the love of life and quest for meaning there as well as the hunger for right relationships. Further, well-attended religious services sponsored by the Metropolitan Community Church, Dignity, Integrity and other Protestant, Orthodox, and Jewish groups testify to the vitality of that religious sensitivity Jung had recognized so many years ago. In fact, the national and international networks of such religious organizations represent the largest gay organizations in the world.

JUSTICING

Gerard Manley Hopkins' telling phrase "The just man justices" (from "Kingfishers Catch Fire") grasps the essential meaning of the thing. Justice is an active effort to bring about right relationships in every area of life, to inaugurate the Kingdom of Heaven. The heart of justice is compassion — the ability to care for others, in particular those who suffer. Among gay men and women, who have certainly tasted the gall of political, economic, and religious oppression, compassion should come easily and justicing follow as a matter of course.

Today, few countries still prosecute gays for private, consensual behavior between adults, the United States being one of the few, but discrimination continues. It is thus not surprising that much of the justicing of the gay community concerns liberation. But gays cannot afford to limit their concern to themselves. For all minority groups are necessarily linked in a common struggle for *human* rights — not gay rights, black rights, women's rights, Indian rights, Chicano rights, or old people's rights, but the fundamental rights of *all* people.

Active solidarity among gay men and women and other minorities is the kind of political expression of faith that a contemporary spirituality must enhance.[11] Minimally, it calls for active participation in the ordinary political process and the fulfillment of civic responsibilities, guided by a radical love of freedom and human dignity.

THE SPIRIT OF FRIENDSHIP

The great psychologist C. G. Jung was keenly aware of the spiritual potential of homosexuality concerning affection, (non-erotic) friendship among members of the same gender and even between men and women, who are so often antagonists in the psycho-social warfare of the sexes. Homosexuality, he wrote, referring specifically but not exclusively to male homosexuality, "gives him a great capacity for friendship, which often creates ties of astonishing tenderness between men, and may even rescue friendship between the sexes from its limbo of the impossible.[12]

The greatest and for that reason the most challenging dimension of human life is the achievement and development of true friendships. Love in its wide sense is not only the deepest and most universal of all human values, it is in loving that we discover most directly in our experience what *God* means. Human loves are the sacrament of our love for and by God. Friendship as inclusive love, "unconditional positive regard," is the nucleus of all spirituality, condensing all aspects of corporeality, consciousness, and social concern into one act of integration. Love is not only our most radical capacity for transcendence, it becomes real only as we actually reach out and join with others, beyond ourselves and yet within ourselves, that is, as One Self: "You in me and I in you" (John 14:20).

Love is ultimately One but not one-dimensional. It is the poet's "many-splendored thing." C.S. Lewis wrote of "four loves" — sexual love, affection, friendship, and charity.[13] But these are really four *ways* of loving, each a manifestation of a certain dimension of human love. For gay men and women, as for everyone else, spirituality integrates all the various loves of our lives, developing the art of loving appropriately to the situation in which we and our loved ones discover each other. Not all loves will be erotic, not all affectionate or amicable. All can, however, be expressions of charity — *agape* — which binds all the others together.

So harmonized, all our loves will first of all be *transcendent* — an escape from the prison of self-centeredness, and therefore *ek-static* — a going-out-of-ourselves to others. Secondly, our loves will be *inclusive* — not actually including everyone in particular, which only God could encompass in the divine sweep of an infinite solicitude — but extended towards everyone we meet. Again, the ways of loving will vary concretely — erotic love will probably be the most restrictive, because of its very intensity. Affection and friendship will extend outward much farther. But *agape* does in effect open us to all creation — it is non-exclusive love, God's love loving through us. It is a general, universal love, particularized by each actual encounter, and only as restricted in the long haul as is our experience itself.

With regard to gay love, what is important to note here is that it will extend outward inclusively, from the intimacy of *eros* to the openness of *agape*. And while *eros* may well be limited to those of the same sex, the other loves are not, and must not be cut short by "heterophobia." The most pressing danger to gay men and women who do not associate with the opposite sex except by necessity is that the feeling, even the attitude, that the "other" sex is superfluous may become a fact.

The complementary of the sexes is not primarily a matter of physiology. Psychologically and socially, having real friends of the opposite sex(es) is *necessary* to activate the bisexual personality components in every man and woman, which is to say, for true sexual integration. Suppressing either aspect of sexuality distorts our personality and our experience of life. It produces psychological and social imbalance. That bias is both reflected in and engineered by the exclusion of "the others" from one's circle of friends, whether because of fear, hostility, or plain indifference.

For gay men and women (and for straight people as well), it is therefore spiritually necessary to have not only gay friends of both sexes, but straight friends of both sexes as well. The lesbian unable to relate to straight women is no more healthy and integrated than a straight women unable to relate to lesbians. The same holds true equally for gay and straight men. The relative proportions of male and female, gay and straight friends will vary for every person; the main issue is that each of us needs to know the rest of us, and by knowing, to learn how to love one another better in both our sameness and our differences.

NOTES

1. There have been several recent efforts to explicitate a spirituality which takes into consideration the special exigencies of lesbian and gay experience, among them Norman Pittenger, *Gay Lifestyles: A Christian Interpretation of Homosexuality and the Homosexual*, Los Angeles: The Universal Fellowship Press, 1977, Barbara Zanotti, ed., *A Faith of One's Own: Explorations by Catholic Lesbians*, Trumansburg, NY: The Crossing Press, 1986; see also Matthew Fox, "The Spiritual Journey of the Homosexual... and Just about Everybody Else," in Nugent, op. cit., pp. 189-204, James D. Whitehead and Evelyn Eaton Whitehead, "Three Passages of Maturity," ibid., pp. 174-188, and Bruce Williams, "Gay Catholics and Eucharistic Communion: Theological Parameters," ibid., pp. 205-15.
2. See *The Center of the Cyclone*, New York: Bantam Books, 1973, and *The Programming and Metaprogramming of the Human Biocomputer*, New York: Julian Press, 1972.
3. Cf. Arthur C. Deikman, "Deautomatization and the Mystic Experience," *Psychiatry* 29 (1966): 324-38. Cf. also Peter Berger and Thomas Luckmann, *The Social Construction of Reality*, Garden City, NY: Doubleday, 1967.
4. Cf. Kenneth Wapnick, "Mysticism and Schizophrenia," *Journal of Transpersonal Psychology* 1, 2 (Fall 1969): 49-66, and Roland Fischer, "A Cartography of Ecstatic and Meditative States," *Science* 174, 4012 (26 Nov. 1971): 897-904.
5. C.G. Jung, *The Collected Works*, trans. by R.F.C. Hull, New York: Pantheon, 1959, Vol. 9, p. 87. I am indebted to Fr. John McNeill for bringing this passage to my attention.
6. Cf. Mircea Eliade, *Shamanism*, New York: Pantheon, 1964. For an overview of such evidence, see Karlen, op. cit., pp. 464-65 and 639-40. For an extensive and recent discussion, see Mark Thompson, ed., *Gay Spirit: Myth and Meaning*, New York: St. Martin's Press, 1987, passim.

7. Cf. *Man's Body* by the Diagram Group, New York: Bantam Books, 1977, pp. H-1 to 52, and for a discussion of drug use among gays, Mark Freedman and Harvey Mayes, *Loving Man*, New York: Hark Publishing Col, pp. 115-20. Vincent Virga's *A Comfortable Corner* (New York: Avon, 1986) is a sensitive novel which deals with problems of gay alcoholism, love, and friendship. For an excellent discussion of the connection between substance-abuse, health, and AIDS, see Tom O'Connor, *Living with AIDS*, op. cit. pp. 94-100.

8. Cf. Freedman, "Far from Illness: Homosexuals May Be Healthier than Straights," art. cit. For discussion, see above, pp. 15f.

9. On meditation, see William Johnston, S.J., *Silent Music*, New York: Harper & Row, 1976; Lawrence LeShan, *How to Meditate*, New York: Bantam Books, 1974; Claudio Naranjo and Robert Ornstein, *The Psychology of Meditation*, New York: Viking, 1971; Thomas Merton, *Contemplative Prayer*, Garden City, NY: Doubleday Image Books, 1971, and *Contemplation in a World of Action*, Garden City, NY: Doubleday Image Books, 1973.

10. A classic work in this area is still James B. Nelson's *Embodiment*, Minneapolis: Augsburg Publishing Co., 1978.

11. For a further discussion of the political implications of spirituality, see *The Mystical and Political Dimensions of the Christian Faith*, Claude Geffre and Gustavo Gutierrez, eds. (Concilium, Vol. 96), New York: Herder & Herder, 1974.

12. Loc. cit., p. 86. For an insightful commentary on this passage, cf. John McNeill, S.J., *The Church and the Homosexual*, pp. 137ff.

13. C.S. Lewis, *The Four Loves*, New York: Harcourt, Brace, Jovanovich, 1960.

CHAPTER EIGHT

Resistance

ALL Christian spirituality has a positive and a negative side. For while fundamentally optimistic about the radical goodness of the world and especially of its human inhabitants (Gen. 1:1-31), Christians have never long deceived themselves about the "brokenness" of that world, including the tendency in all of us toward sin — both individually and collectively. Christianity takes evil seriously, but not too seriously.

Much of the preliminary phases of Christian spirituality as the art of integral living has a negative tone, then, because it recognizes the necessity of confronting the real evil in us and around us. More accurately, there are *therapeutic* aspects of spirituality which concentrate on healing the wounds of sin and overcoming the brokenness of the world. Only to that extent *can* spirituality be re-integrative, poised against the forces of disintegration from within and without. But the main thrust of Christian spirituality remains positive and, as such, developmental. It aims at fostering growth, once destructive agencies have been identified and the process of resistance begun.

As Christian, gay spirituality will also have a negative aspect — one of resistance, protest, and reform which addresses the destructive forces of the gay world perhaps even more than those stemming from the fear, ignorance, and prejudice of straight society. But also as Christian, even a minimally adequate gay spirituality will possess a more fundamental and positive emphasis on growth toward the full humanness of a mature and creative faith.

For most gays, including those who recognize themselves as God's friends, the challenges they face both from the straight world and from their own world can be summed up as a diminishment of self-worth, the relentless if not always overt prejudice and discrimination they meet in daily life, a lack of meaning — both being misunderstood and their own failure to grasp the meaning of life — and, finally, the manipulation and exploitation based on their sexual orientation.

The miracle of gay life is not that there are not failures and tragedies, for there are, but that there is so much love, laughter, and health in the gay world, to paraphrase Evelyn Hooker. The courage and resilience of gays is not just the embattled defiance of a besieged minority group, but a strength that derives from profound human resources and subtle perceptiveness "well-seasoned with wit" (Col. 4:6). From a spiritual viewpoint, gay men and women live in a situation in which they must constantly reaffirm the meaning and value of life or be thrown back into confusion, hopelessness, and estrangement. One of the greatest values gays offer to society in a broken world is the sense of human value itself.

Evil exists in the gay world as well as around it; resisting sin and evil thus warrants consideration here. For the positive elements of Christian spirituality provide a response to personal sinfulness as well as to sinful social structures.

SIN AND EVIL IN THE GAY WORLD

When Dr. Martin Hoffman subtitled his study of male homosexuality "the social creation of evil," he touched on the nerve which, from a religious viewpoint, is possibly the most sensitive of all. Few groups in modern society are so encapsulated by morally destructive social forces as the gay community. In large measure, the very existence of a gay world is a product of social evil: fear, ignorance, and persecution from straight society and exploitation and degradation arising from within the ghetto. The successes of gay men and lesbians in resisting these truly demonic powers by living according to positive ethical norms, as well as by Christian moral values in many cases, testify to a persistent spiritual strength. It also points to what I think is the major ministry of Christian gays — the redemption of the gay world itself, by authentic witness and by creating alternatives to the morally destructive forces and structures in that world.

The distinctive Christian awareness of sin is not only realistic but healthy, because human evil is a real dimension of every person's experience apart from all questions of determinism. We may not be able to eliminate sin altogether. But we can overcome it. Sin in this sense means the failure to realize ultimate values in everyday actions, as well as manifest violations of moral norms. As responsible persons we all have to acknowledge as honestly as we can the sins we commit or condone. But it is important to remember that we also have an equal, even prior responsibility to know when we are *not* sinning.

One of the major blindnesses of moralists in considering homosexuality (and sexuality in general) has been the failure to see that the central problem of sin and evil is not the "rectitude" of individual, physical acts, but the structural forces of the societal systems in which men and women must live. These contextual elements, truly sinful social structures, must be recognized as precipitating factors in the moral struggle of gays and lesbians.

Further, real sin and guilt must be discerned in terms of the fundamental attitude of the individual person toward other persons, toward himself or herself, and toward God. The "essence" of sin in the personal sphere is the elevation of *myself* to an all-important status, so that everyone, or, more accurately, *any*one is reduced to the status of an object for my desire or use without regard to his or her dignity, needs, desires, or well-being. Sin is not just selfishness, but also "otherlessness." Ultimately, it is the failure to love, whether by refusal or by violation.

Thus, the sexual "sins" of teenagers (in particular) and many adults should not be seen so much as disordered acts or the experience of forbidden pleasure as the failure to treat themselves and others with the care and love they deserve.

Several individual problem areas have already been considered in previous chapters, and there is little need here for more than a summary. Most moral difficulties fall into three main groups:

Personal diminishment: "ontological" guilt — the belief that gay is bad and therefore that gays are sick and evil. Insecurity, dependency, passiveness. Escapism — fantasy and isolationism. Materialism.

Sexual irresponsibility: Self-indulgence, infidelity, obsessive preoccupation with genital sexuality, trivialization of sex, promiscuity, sado-masochism.

Interpersonal falseness: "games," evasiveness, affectation, stereotyped behavior, superficiality, deception, fickleness, dishonesty, betrayal.

There are also particular temptations of members of any subgroup, especially an oppressed minority. Among them, I would first list the tendency to deify its virtues and ignore its faults. *Idealization* is a fancier name for it — the process by which the underdog triumphs over its adversaries by wishful thinking. The attempt to live up to a merely ideal image can be either comical or grotesque. The *macho* male, an image so prevalent among young Latinos, is a caricature of masculinity. But when acted out, it produces vicious results: the degradation of women, the brutalization of men, artificiality, games, the perpetuation of a destructive sexual mythology. "Homosexualism" — the mystique that "gay is best" — is no less a caricature than *machismo*. It is also no less destructive and degrading.

The plunge into *ideology*, a natural aftermath of a dip into idealization, represents a falsification of thinking to justify a destructive or unauthentic life-style — a kind of rationalization. Allowing patterns of behavior to influence thought patterns to the extent of losing the capacity for independent decision-making and action is humanly injurious to anyone. This is one reason why we all need to be able to "unwind," and just "be ourselves." Otherwise, social roles tend to become permanent identities, and here gay life can be a particularly dangerous trap. Escaping the enforced masquerade of the daytime business world into the nocturnal gay world can be a mere shift from one set of artificialities to another. The natural self tends to get lost somewhere between.

Labeling represents a form of ideological strategy which has few if any beneficial aspects. Being typed, especially as a social deviant, and whether by oneself or others, carries with it not only a degree of stigmatization, but a set of action-expectancies. A labeled person is expected to behave in a certain fashion, which is taken to typify the whole class. Usually, the behavior comes about one way or another by the curious dynamics of the "self-fulfilling prophecy" — once a thief, always a thief. Labeling further permits society (i.e., other people) to deal with "deviants" (i.e., trouble-makers, dissidents) in short order, most simply by dismissing them as "bums," "queers," "dykes," "yuppies," "commies," or what-have-you.

Before accepting or adopting the label "homosexual" or even "gay," it is advisable to consider carefully the kind of expectations, limitations, and attitudes that are attached to the label.[1] Coming out can be restrictive as well as liberating, both in and out of the ghetto. "Gay" is not merely a verbal tag to which people are indifferent.

It seems to me that straight people (not just heterosexual persons, but "non-deviants" in general) will tolerate a good deal of so-called deviance in others so long as the "different" social behavior, including sexual conduct, is kept private, that is, devoid of public attention, banners, placards, and slogans. Or labels. It is important to bear in mind that avoiding being labeled is vastly different from either staying in the closet or "passing" as straight. It simple means being yourself. If *that* isn't acceptable, labeling won't help.

Conversely, the straight world's resistance to labeling is

highly selective and can be a forceful way of preventing constructive confrontation. As long as blacks could be called Negroes, black pride and black power could be kept at bay, psychologically and socially. Similarly, either by keeping gay men and women safely in the closet, or by perpetuating formal labels such as "homosexual," the challenge of gay pride and gay power can be avoided. Dismissing them as "fairies" or "fags" is as short a step as it was from Negro to "nigger."

Despite its moral and psychological demands, however, coming out can be a forceful way of instituting social change by initiating a change in consciousness, first among gays themselves, then among straight people. A person may have valid reasons for not coming out "all the way," but there are equally valid and perhaps more urgent reasons for strategic public acknowledgment. But no one should be forced to come out, whether by straight pressure or by that of gay militancy.

SOCIAL SIN

It is temptingly easy to harp on the social immorality of the gay world as it is to rant about the alleged depravity of individuals. But it could be equally foolish to ignore the immense problems presented to gays by their partially created, partially inherited environment — a moral climate which, for good or ill, cannot be completely avoided even by gays who have little to do with the ghetto and its sub-cultural excrescences — films, magazines, hardware, etc.

Many of these have already been mentioned, others need little comment: the rejection and abandonment of gays by gays, the depreciation of the aged, ugly, and "ungifted," the epidemic of venereal diseases, and AIDS itself. Fundamentally, the sinful social elements in the gay world fall into two major classes: immoral environmental institutions and exploitation. The negative impact of bars, baths, and films, as well as cruising, tricking, etc., has been traced before. Most of these and other environmental factors can be summed up under one rubric: pornography.

THE SEX TRIP: PORN

Pornography is not merely vicarious "sex thrills" packaged in cheap plastic, but a mentality that is both pervasive and subtle. It is the belief that human sexuality and thus human persons are cheap, vile, and marketable.

Porn is perhaps the most insidious enemy gays face — the deep, secret fear that despite all the liberal rhetoric sex is not only dirty, but evil. It is not so much said as lived. Sexual contact among homosexual males (especially) is too often a matter of anonymous encounters, whether in public washrooms, steam baths, casual pick-ups in parks and on beaches, or terminal one-night stands following a chance meeting at a gay bar or theater. Such furtive, often commercial, and hastily forgotten experiences are not just the result of straight oppression, for they persist in areas where consensual sexual activities in private are not illegal.

Much of the message of gay magazines and newspapers, and films, as well as the environment of the bars and baths, only reinforces such a pornographic conception of sex — not, of course, an explicit avowal that it is evil and sinful, ideas alien to gay culture and media, but that sex (or, rather, orgasm) is a constant and undeniable need and therefore a right which must be satisfied as frequently and easily as possible.

Any human activity voluntarily pursued under conditions of anonymity, haste, darkness, and the fear of being caught or even seen hardly signifies psychological or moral healthiness. To the extent that an intolerant and repressive society has contributed to these conditions, the society itself is pornographic, as Dr. Hoffman insisted. Those caught up in it may be more pitiable than worthy of prosecution. But the overall situation cannot be accounted for merely in terms of reaction. And to attempt to glorify or justify the situation is far more pathological than merely being victimized by it.

"SEXPLOITATION"

In every restricted social group, there will be people both eager to be of service and those ready to exploit that limited sphere for everything they can get from it. It should not be surprising that along with gay counseling services, legal aid programs, health clinics, benevolent associations, and religious missions there are also brothels, bars, baths, porn shops, and other establishments that range from mildly parasitic to vampirical. Many of these institutions exploit gays by promoting activities that not only pay well but encourage compulsive behavior.

Few if any of even the most dehumanizing institutions in the gay ghetto lack their counterparts in the straight world, of course. Nevertheless, what makes the situation more oppressive and tragic in the ghetto is that the endless exploitation of an already socially oppressed minority is being engineered by gays themselves who are only too willing to make a dollar out of the skins of their comrades. It is also true that not all recreational establishments that cater to gays are equally or even deliberately exploitative, and some have positive aspects. Most, however, seem prone to advertise in terms of the lowest common denominator in the gay world: the promise of easy sex.

THE POWER OF RESISTANCE

Specific forms of resistance against personal diminishment, sexual irresponsibility, and interpersonal falseness can be as simply enumerated as were their opposites: honest self-evaluation and acceptance; discipline, restraint and altruism; fidelity and constancy; realism about oneself and the gay scene as well as the straight world; empathy and compassion for straights as well as gays; openness, simplicity, truthfulness; and commitment to growth. Social challenges require action as well as character, among them legal reform and education, protest against intramural exploitation, and the creation of alternatives for meeting and recreation.

The power of pornography can be effectively overcome not by a puritanical "Aunt Nancy" mentality which swoons at the mention of sex and which is thus no less pornographic, but rather by a truly humane and Christian attitude toward sexuality. The authentic Christian vision is based solidly on the conviction, laboriously achieved through entries of experience, that sex is neither shameful nor sinful, but morally excellent and spiritually ennobling, a gift and thus a grace which in its true human enjoyment brings men and women into the creative mystery of God's life and love.[2]

In regard to sexual exploitation, similarly, it is one thing to disapprove of the baths, beaches, and bushes for oneself, but what of others? Keeping *your* head together in a bar with a bad reputation counts for little if your presence there constitutes a tacit recommendation for others. Moreover, your patronization contributes financially to the further exploitation of your gay brothers and sisters.

Creating alternatives to the dehumanizing sexual circuses of the baths and other institutions of exploitation will accomplish little if the existence of such establishments continues without any kind of resistance or criticism from within the gay community. For example, not long ago on the east coast, a gay bar notorious for its exploitative activities was successfully picketed by militant gay liberation forces. Such liberation can be achieved, and should be, by gays themselves, who can afford to be nor more tolerant of gay exploitation and the "soft" oppression it represents than they are of straight persecution.

MORAL GROWTH AND THE DISCIPLINE OF LOVE

Traditional Christian references to the qualities of moral strength and behavior have been so abused and disemboweled by pettiness and Jansenistic body-phobias that the very words "virtue," "chastity," "purity," and "modesty" evoke mainly comic sentiments or anger.

Chastity simply means the responsible and creative expression of our God-given sexual capacities for mutual fulfillment — physically, psychologically, and spiritually. Christian sexuality involves, as a consequence, fidelity, sensitivity to the needs, moods, and abilities of the other, mutual generosity, respect, and integrity. Such a contextual understanding of sexuality also implies a foundation of permanent commitment, constancy, and trust.[3]

Discipline and restraint have been traditionally (and wisely) identified as the necessary conditions for the responsible expression of sexuality, especially in terms of genital relations. Known to the ancient world as *modestia* or "moderateness," such active control is called for in several important areas of life, even those lacking an immediate connection with genital behavior. In a brilliant phenomenological analysis of sexual behavior, St. Thomas Aquinas pointed out four: recreation, dress, self-esteem, and curiosity (cf. his *Summa Theologiae*, II-II, QQ. 160-161, 166-169).

Moderation in recreation means acquiring the kind of self-control over our gestures and behavior which most people identify with good manners. Thomas insists that play and recreation are necessary for a balanced life — jokes, light conversation, and games, including athletics, are mainly what he had in mind. For Thomas, *modestia* in this area is expressed as friendliness or affability — a positive regard for others marked by the avoidance of injury, sarcasm, obscenity, and excess.

From a Christian perspective, this recalls Paul's suggestion to the Colossians (3:8f): "You must give up being angry, bad-tempered, spiteful, using abusive language and dirty talk; and never tell each other lies." (Cf. also Phil. 4:8 and Eph. 5:3-5.) The touchstone here with respect to sexuality is a pre-occupation with genital behavior as a topic of conversation and jokes. And in the gay world, the immediate context is camp, gossip, and sexist language.

While generally innocuous, camp can easily become destructive when directed against someone in a malicious way, or even if intended as good-natured "dishing," when it causes embarrassment, humiliation, or offense. Camp can also substitute for open and intimate conversation, becoming a verbal game that is both evasive and manipulative, whether by merely keeping conversation on a trivial level of puns and innuendo, or by tightly controlling the direction and depth of the dialogue. Another problem camp creates through double-entendres and oblique comments is the strict, if not sharp, focus on sex, which further strengthens the preoccupation with the mating details which tie much of gay society together verbally.

The close connections and sense of solidarity in the gay world permit a good deal of talk about what (or whom) people are doing — probably the most common topic of any gay conversation. The combination of a highly effective grapevine with an insatiable interest in everyone's affairs produces a tough brand of gossip. Not all gossip is destructive, but accounts of affairs, break-ups, and breakdowns very easily cross over from "newsflash" to detraction and calumny. And besides the loss of reputation implicit in the dynamics of gossip, there are other problems: the betrayal of the confidences, trust, and secrets without which intimacy and friendship can hardly exist. Gossip also functions as a leveling mechanism, quickly whittling down anyone considered to have "pretensions."

A final talk-trap associated with camp is the use (mainly if not exclusively, by males) of cross-gender references. While it may be superficially just "campy" to refer, for instance, to a man as "she," such inversions indicate deeper, more problematic attitudes, specifically a sexist bias. For feminine pronouns and nicknames are used basically *as* camp — for comic effect, mild irony, and sometimes vicious verbal abuse. But never in anything but a condescending manner. Authentic liberation in the gay world demands the eradication of such degrading patronization of both women and men.

REGALIA

Thomas also discusses moderation in dress — a particularly important area in the lives of many gays, especially those who enjoy the bar scene and late night comraderie in the ghetto. Cruising has much to do with dress, of course, and in addition to clothing itself, keys, handkerchiefs, chains, and almost anything wearable can be used to signal availability and preference. Modesty in clothing is thus not merely a matter of not arousing people by accentuating the sexual organs, buttocks, and breasts, but also concerns an excessive interest in clothing for reasons of vanity and ostentation. (A studied *lack* of care about clothing can be just as effective a way of attracting attention.) Beyond "leading someone on," a preoccupation with clothes, jewelry, cosmetics, scents, hair-styles, the proper shade of tan, and the right pose can too easily replace care for the deeper elements of personality, as mentioned before.

A merely compensating concern with appearance typical of some gay men and lesbians (as well as most other people), is hardly worth caviling over. But there is the likelihood that things will not end in mere compensation, which *is* worth a word. From a Christian perspective, the body should be cultivated, celebrated, and adorned as the house of the Spirit as well as the manifest, personal "you." "Looking good" is a way of showing respect and care for others, too. But moderation in dress and grooming is necessary for balance, both mental and spiritual, just as it is in art and architecture.

SELF-ESTEEM AND RESPECT FOR OTHERS

St. Thomas' main concern with *modestia* is not merely with clothes and raunchy behavior. The kinds of moderation he especially emphasizes are proper self-esteem and intellectual simplicity — what medieval writers called humility and studiosity. *Humilitas* means having a modest opinion of yourself — that is, a true estimate of your own worth, without the embroidery of pretense, exaggerated self-regard, *or* self-depreciation.

Whatever "studiosity" brings to mind today, Thomas' fourth kind of *modestia* counters the tendency toward unbridled curiosity, which is not a mere eagerness to know, but a desire to know too much. The insatiable desire to know it all, especially about people, leads to snooping, prying, and considerable wasted energy, as well as tending towards harmful gossip.

An ethic of moderation in behavior, dress, self-reference, and people-interests may, indeed *will*, appear to many as a quaint and puritanical holdover from some sexually repressive period of history. The mordant observations of Thomas Aquinas and his sources indicate just the contrary; they knew what they were talking about and their remarks still, almost curiously, strike home. (Aristotle: "It is a mark of effeminacy to let one's cloak trail on the ground to avoid the trouble of lifting it up.")

From a psychological point of view, one not absent from Thomas' thinking, the restraint implied in *modestia* has an important function in a cultural situation in which the glorification of sex has reached heights as idolatrous as any in past ages. Restraint means being self-possessed, liberated from the competitive tyranny of the sexual meat-market. Avoidance of some places and persons will probably be necessary for many in order to retain the basic self-respect which should characterize an integrated person. But from a Christian point of view, the ability to conduct oneself responsibly in an irresponsible situation rather than retreating from it has the added value of witness and example. Not the pharisaical self-righteousness which can simply substitute for other forms of sexual gamesmanship, but the lived testimony of a balanced, playful, but inner-directed person. A real Christian presence is redemptive, but not obtrusive. It should convey a sense of freedom to those around, not one of inhibition.

St. Paul certainly had something like this in mind when he encouraged the Christians of Philippi "to act in everything you do without grumbling or argument; prove yourselves innocent and straightforward, children of God beyond reproach in the midst of a twisted and depraved generation — among whom you shine like the stars in the sky" (Phil. 2:14-15). He concludes, "Let your *modestia* be evident to everyone" (4:5). To the Colossians he wrote, similarly, "Conduct yourselves intelligently with those who are not Christians, and make the best use of your time. Keep your conversation pleasant and flavored with wit [literally, 'salty'] so that you will know best how to respond to each person" (4:5-6).

The Forgotten Option

The ordinary opinion of moral theologians in the past was that among possible life-ways open to homosexual men and women, celibacy — the state of dedicated singleness, that is, total abstinence from any active sex-life — was the only acceptable choice. Recently, theological voices have raised the possibility of a responsible expression of sexuality for those outside the married state in special circumstances: widows, single men and women, and gay and lesbian couples. Recognized moralists have also countenanced permanent homosexual relationships as a "lesser evil" than a life of promiscuity for gays when celibacy is not a live option.[4]

While I am not sure that "lesser evil" is an appropriate designation for a faithful, constant, and loving human relationship, I wish here to suggest that celibacy, too, should be given thoughtful consideration as an authentic and fully responsible life-style for gays insofar as it represents a free decision.

As a Christian life-style, celibacy must be freely chosen for the sake of the Kingdom of Heaven as a response to a call from God recognized by the Church either publicly or privately. It would be an abuse of language to tag as celibate the irresponsible bachelorhood of the straight or gay "swinger," even though it may well be a freely chosen state. Likewise to call celibate the enforced state of criminals, the required state of military cadets, or the involuntary condition of being unmarried, would be confusing and wrong-headed.

Celibacy as a responsible expression of sexuality is not fundamentally a mere "discipline" in the Roman Catholic Church. It is a spiritual, indeed *mystical* identification with Christ, who, as the coming Lord, transcends the structures of this world, including marriage. (Married love also has an "eschatological" character in the unselfish commitment of husband and wife, who embody in their mutual love God's love for his people in Christ — see Eph. 5:21-33.) Significantly, without the manifest relation of the freely accepted renunciation of marriage and genital sexuality for the sake of the Kingdom, the single state has no specific Christian value as such, and if involuntary, represents an unfortunate human situation.[5]

"Celibacy" as the enforced state of singleness many churchmen would require of all homosexual Christians as a necessary consequence of their sexual orientation is also anything but a free response to a grace of God. It is more punitive than the forced deprivation of convicts, who are sometimes allowed to marry even while imprisoned. Such a demand differs radically from both the celibacy of priests and religious as well as those lay persons who take private vows, for it takes no account of either the desire of the person or his or her ability to live celibately — a situation unthinkable for candidates for the priesthood, the religious life, or for those who choose to live celibately in the world. (In fact, the alleged *inability* of gays to observe celibacy is one reason recently adduced for refusing them entrance to the priesthood and religious life!)

The practice of forced celibacy is clearly at odds with traditional Christian theology. The alternative, of course, is to recognize as valid for gay Christians a way of life, if not tantamount to marriage, at least open to some form of sexual expression. This the church has been unwilling to do, and thus arises the dilemma of the Christian, gay *or* straight, for whom neither celibacy nor marriage are psychologically, personally, or spiritually desirable or even possible.

Celibacy should remain a real option for Christian gays, however, whether in the priesthood, the religious life, or as a consecrated life-style in the world. Homosexuality cannot *require* grace, which is essentially a free gift; it can, however, be an occasion for grace. And despite the occasional bias of vocation directors, novice mistresses, pessimistic bishops, and seminary rectors, it is quite evident that many homosexual priests, deacons, sisters, and brothers are serving God's people faithfully, responsibly, and celibately throughout the world.

IN SPIRIT AND TRUTH

The most urgent matter at issue which gays need to address is neither theological nor political, but spiritual. A shift in political positions or theological understanding without a corresponding advancement in spirituality would be shallow. Moreover, as a cohesive and motivating force, a spiritual breakthrough should accelerate the process of theological and political liberation, and it will also provide reserves of strength when setbacks occur. Furthermore, the Church as a whole is undergoing a crisis of spirituality, in no small part due to the irresistible fragmentation produced by the confrontation between Christianity and the modern world. More than ever in an increasingly interdependent world society there is a need today for diverse Christian spiritualities applicable to particular situations and groups.

As mentioned in the preceding chapter, gay spirituality will be rooted primarily in the gospel of Jesus Christ. That is, it will be radically Christian, more indebted to faith in Christ than reliant on spiritualities of the past few centuries. A vital spirituality always develops in the encounter between the Spirit of Christ and the emergence of a new situation or group in the church. Gays are such a group today, despite the fact that there have always been homosexual Christians, because our understanding of homosexuality has changed more radically in the last twenty years than in the previous twenty centuries.

As full members of the Church, gay Christians must also appropriate the spiritual inheritance of the whole Christian people, especially as recorded in the lives of its saints and

mystics.   There are, however, no autobiographies of gay saints
— at least none known as such.   (Responsible scholars have
established that several outstanding Christian figures, many of
them saints, were most likely homosexual, including St.
Sebastian, Sts. Cosmas and Damian, Gerard Manley Hopkins,
and Dag Hammarskjold.)   As *gay* saints, today's men and
women must write their own spiritual autobiographies, aided
by mutual sharing and reflection.   Their stories may some day
be a source of inspiration and guidance for other gay Christians
as the writings of Augustine, Francis of Assisi, and Dorothy Day
have been for countless persons.

Spiritually, the experience of gay Christians constitutes a
virtual model of radical faith according to the mind of St. Paul
and reaffirmed by Augustine, Luther, and the Protestant
tradition: we are saved solely by God's grace through faith.
There is nothing we *can* do to justify ourselves and thus merit
salvation; thus, there is nothing we *need* to do — except to accept
the love, forgiveness, and grace of God as it comes to us in the
manifold experiences of life.   And *then* act accordingly!

Here the existential element of spirituality surfaces and leads
us to the mystical and prophetic dimension of gay life.   To the
sometimes awful and painful cry, "Why me?" there comes a
reply, not so much in words as in an experience of free
acceptance by God.   As one young gay man wrote to me:
"When I started attending Mass again after my separation from
the church, I prayed to Christ while looking at the large crucifix
above the altar.   The prayer was simple: 'Are you for real and
there for me?'   During Holy Week services a couple of years
ago, I got my answer.   I said my little prayer as always but this
time Jesus looked down at me and said: 'Yes, I am real and I
know about your being gay, but I don't care.   My love is for
you, too.'   I went home and cried."

For many lesbians and gay men, the turn inwards (and
outwards) towards a deeper spirituality may come either as a
gesture of desperation in the face of life's absurdities, or as the
consummation of a life of struggle, sacrifice, and dedication.   It
may just happen as the final development of a natural process of

maturing. But it need not be delayed until the end of life, nor should it be. For an adequate spirituality can provide the integrating power a lesbian or gay man needs throughout life to resist the forces of disintegration pressing in from both the straight world in the form of repression, and from the gay world as exploitation. Beyond resistance, spirituality also provides the integrating focus through which a life acquires meaning, dignity, and value.

NOTES

1. Cf. John P. de Cecco, ed., *Gay Personality and Sexual Labeling*, New York: Harrington Park Press, 1985.
2. The common teaching of the Church, this view of sexuality has been recently articulated by Christian writers such as Dr. Jack Dominian, Rev. Norman Pittenger, and Joan Timmerman in terms applicable to both heterosexual and homosexual Christians. See Resources for Further Study, pp. 181ff.
3. On chastity, see the chapter on sexuality and mysticism in Richard Woods, *Mysterion: An Approach to Mystical Spirituality*, Chicago: Thomas More Press, 1981. See also John Macmurray, *Reason and Emotion*, London: Faber and Faber, 1967.
4. See above, pp. 58, 105, 108, 119, n. 6.
5. For a treatment of celibacy still remarkable for its insight and compassion, see especially Edward Schillebeeckx, *Celibacy*, New York: Sheed and Ward, 1968.

CHAPTER NINE

The Joy of Being Gay

A favorite device of anti-gay politicians, religious figures, and psychotherapists, is to challenge and belittle the very word "gay," claiming, as in a recent book, that the author has never encountered a truly happy homosexual.[1] At least part of the problem is that such authors' clients ordinarily come to them for help precisely because they are troubled, fearful, and unhappy. That hardly means everyone else is! I suspect that a larger part of the difficulty comes from the authors' antecedent belief that there *cannot* be any joy in being gay. The dilemma reminds me of a bitterly prejudiced policewoman I knew who despised black people as a whole because many of the criminals she arrested were black.

I can testify from nearly twenty years of sexual counseling and spiritual direction that just as there is plenty of health, so also there is plenty of joy in being gay, both in individual lives and in public convocations such as Dignity masses, conventions, and Gay Pride Week festivities. The discovery by Bell and Weinberg that close-bonded gay and lesbian couples tended to be generally happier than their straight counterparts should be considered with special care before consigning gay men and women to the weeping and gnashing section of society.[2] Or of the Kingdom of Heaven. There is plenty of suffering and sadness in the gay world, far more than there should be. There is also a lot of surface "gaiety," whistling in the dark, and wishful thinking. But there is also a surprising surplus of true love, profound happiness, and real joy.

Sunday, June 27, 1976. No one has ever heard of AIDS....
Gay Pride Week is drawing to a close with the annual parade
and rally. Hundreds of gays and lesbians are already marching
as I arrive. Some are on floats, some astride cars, a few on roller
skates and skate boards. Thousands of spectators line both
sides of Broadway. There is little heckling and no violence.
Many gays exchange campy wisecracks and banter with the
spectators. As I glance over the crowd it makes sense —
perhaps a third of the people on the street are wearing gay pride
buttons or other identifying tags.

Banners, tee-shirts, and chants herald the various groups:
"Gay and Proud," "Gay Power," "Gay and American," "Two,
four six, eight — we don't overpopulate!" "Hello, padre,"
smiles a Puerto Rican woman as I pass on the sidewalk,
outdistancing the parade. I smile back, wondering if I should
say something.

A large black banner is carried by. The group is from the
Institute of Human Relations, a gay service center. The banner
describes the pink triangle Hitler forced homosexual prisoners
to wear in the concentration camps before slaughtering a
quarter million of them. Pink triangles on black arm-bands are
visible here and there throughout the crowd.

A black man in his early twenties stops me: "Hey, man — do
you believe this?" "It's a fact," I answer, struggling for a reply:
"You don't believe in facts, you accept them." "I've seen this
thing for three years and I *still* don't believe it!" he laughs and
walks on. A huge cloth snake slithers by, green with a black
head and lots of human feet. Its legend: "Don't tread on us!"
Nearby wiggles a Chinese dragon, someone thrusting a popsicle
into its toothy mouth.

The parade will strike me later as an almost perfect model of
the gay world. There are representatives from every element of
the ghetto — female impersonators on cars and floats, some
professional entertainers, others obviously amateur. A couple
of bath houses have elegant floats, as do the more successful
bars — one of them a leather-and-chains pub which caters to the
macho S & M crowd. The men on the float are all in leather, one

strapped to a wooden frame. "Love takes many forms," says a sign. Somewhere else a banner reads, "Ladies, do you know where your husbands are camping tonight?"

Various associations are represented: Mattachine — named for the famous clown figure; One, Inc.; several gay newspapers from Chicago, Milwaukee, and South Bend; and service organizations — Gay Horizons, the Gay Peoples Union, the Human Relations Institute, the Rainbow School for the Deaf, its riders striped with every color conceivable.

The Church is there: MCC has a large delegation with liturgical banners, cars, and a float. Several marchers are wearing clerical collars; they see me, smile and wave. Dignity has a big birthday cake atop one of its cars — a bicentennial theme. One of the chaplains is marching in black suit and collar. Alongside him, a young man who broke his foot three days before is hobbling along on crutches, sweat streaming down his face — it's over ninety degrees. Several marchers see me and wave — a few shout. For a while, I walk with them. It feels odd, uncomfortable at first — but I begin to feel a sense of pride and admiration, as well as an unusual awareness of something else — meaning, point, the scope of it all. I'm not sure what.

After a few minutes, I rejoin the spectators to see the rest of the parade. Integrity is coming up toward the end — a small but brave showing. Once more, a priest is walking with his people, a tall, dignified man, no doubt suffering from the heat, but easily keeping pace with the younger men around him. I wave, but his eyes fixed steadily ahead — he doesn't see me.

Almost at the end of the parade, I see something that I hadn't expected, and my throat constricts — clowns. Over six of them. In full, gaudy costume, their faces painted with huge smiles. They're releasing balloons and chattering with the crowd.

Somewhere a marcher with a black child on his shoulders shouts, "Children are beautiful too...."

At the beginning of this book, my claim that clowns provided a clue to the meaning of being gay perhaps seemed whimsical.

Unpacking that clue is not so much a theological or psychological exercise, but a venture into something more like poetry. It involves a certain view of life, one almost peculiarly Christian: the comic vision. I will now try to explain.

Earlier, I also said that the gay world is a microcosm of the straight world, a kind of model, accentuating both its positive and negative characteristics. As such, the gay world can provide a valuable contribution to the larger society — reflecting its image back, with commentary. In this, the gay world possesses a critical capacity which is all too frequently wasted, that of being a magnifying mirror held before society, particularly with respect to its most often uncritical attitude toward sexuality.

In both the possession of this critical capacity and its failure, gay men and women share a triple vocation: those of the artist, the mystic, and the prophet. The distinct touch of gayness merges this threefold sensitivity to aesthetic value, celebration, and justice into the image of society's mime: the clown. It begins with the ability to see what others do not see, and ends, as William Ernest Hocking said so beautifully, with the will to create through suffering.

THE CREATIVE RESPONSE

It is something of a myth that gays — especially men — are "artsy" people: ballet dancers, interior decorators, hair stylists, actors, window dressers, organists, painters, poets, and so on. But, just as many great athletes and jazz musicians are black, so too many great artists in every field *are* gay — and there is the nucleus of the myth. The great loss to the world of art because of AIDS tragically illustrates the truth of the myth, as well.[3]

Gays have no corner on the arts, of course; most artists are not gay. But the fact that many gays are highly sensitive to aesthetic values and the likelihood that a somewhat disproportionate number of artists and entertainers are gay raises an important question regarding art and homosexuality.

Part of the answer lies, I think, in the openness of the arts to people who may be "different" in many respects but are gifted with artistic capacity. On the other hand, many gays probably gravitate to the arts because of that openness, even those without great artistic talent, content merely to be accepted, if not to shine. But there is, I think, an even deeper reason: the affinity of the artist and the gay person in terms of a fundamental sensitivity tied to a different outlook on the world, one often sharpened to a critical focus by social rejection and personal suffering.

In relation to "straight" society, artists and gay people are misfits and often outcasts, relegated to the fringes of respectability because of the discomfort both their vision of reality and its expression produces in their contemporaries. Frequently, artists behave oddly (as the saints themselves do), driven by their muse, genius, or daimon. They live intensely, drinking life's joys and pains to the dregs, often burning themselves out in the effort to communicate what they have seen to a largely unreceptive world.

Artists have been called the "antennae of the race" because their heightened sensitivities "pick up" meanings and values which the rest of us miss. The social contributions of artists are inestimable in this regard, even apart from the vast and important service they perform in delighting us and awakening us to beauty by reassembling, distilling, or merely pointing to the spectacular richness of human experience in the natural and social world.

It is in this sense that gay men and women are artists of sexuality, for they reveal by their presence, their mere *being*, the meaning and value of human sexuality. Homosexual love does not challenge or inhibit heterosexual love as the normative bond between men and women and the foundation of family life, but distinguishes it and makes it more visible. Without homosexuality as the "beyond" of heterosexuality, much of the significance and worth of heterosexuality might well be swallowed up by the everyday, taken-for-granted ordinariness that pervades our lives.

Thus lesbians and gay men "raise consciousness." Merely being with gays or lesbians comfortable in their own orientation calls straight men and women to question themselves, perhaps not so much consciously as existentially. Men or women uncomfortable with their own sexuality may respond by attacking, just as people uncomfortable with life in general often strike out at artists. Others are less upset, but few are left indifferent.

But gay men and women do not exist merely to heighten people's appreciation of heterosexuality; they no less jarringly propose that male-female relationships can exist on the basis of mere personal attraction, by choice in friendship (*philia*) rather than *eros*, as C. G. Jung suggested. Such a realization is not only beautiful and valuable in itself, it is also liberating, for it also frees us from our fears of same-sex friendships. One of the gravest threats to contemporary civilization is the peculiarly western, male fear that *any* close ties with a person of the same sex is deviant, sick, or immoral. Here, too, gay love, by the contrast of opposition, provides the way out of a trap: close friendship need *not* be a function of sexual magnetism. The cure for homophobia is homophilia.

PROPHECY

Gay sensitivity to the structures and pressures of society, the capacity created by a constant awareness and experience of difference, passes from the artistic to the prophetic as art itself does when it portrays reality truthfully and thereby challenges us to change. For the truth about life is not only its beauty, but its disfigurement and its possibilities; the aesthetic sense becomes a moral sense when it perceives what can and therefore should be.

Social criticism is thus a major contribution of gay existence — again not by actual intention so much as by unavoidable result. Sexual oppression, injustice, prejudice, and discrimination are revealed by the way society treats gays and other despised minorities. All the self-hatred, fear, and doubt of a male-dominated world — both civil and ecclesiastical — has been unleashed at some time against those whose love is so threatening to the masculine mystique. Women's liberation and gay liberation are inseparably linked by being the product by protest of unbridled male domination.

The prophetic aspect of gay experience comes to light particularly in protest against injustice, thus revealing a heightened if perhaps narrow sensitivity to justice. (The limited scope of the justice sought is not detrimental to the true prophetic vocation. If anything, it is characteristic of it, for abstract or general justice is merely an idea or at most a disposition. The prophetic crisis usually involves concrete cases with wider implications; witness Amos and John the Baptist, and, in our own time, Martin Luther King, Jr., Daniel Berrigan, and Steven Biko.)

As the forgotten beauties of love impel the artist to reawaken an automatized society to the meaning of sex and friendship, so the suppressed nobility of justice urges the prophet to call our attention to reform. He or she may do so haltingly and symbolically, like Jeremiah, or with the thunderous eloquence of Savonarola, the power of action of Joan of Arc, the quiet humility of Gandhi, or the courageous dedication of Dorothy Day and Mother Teresa of Calcutta. However it is expressed, the fundamental duty of prophet is to teach — to educate, *e-ducere* — to lead out of darkness into light. And here gay men and women can and must teach both the Church and the State.

The ways of teaching and re-teaching (reformation) are multiple. Passively, gay men and women can educate by permitting bona fide researchers to learn from them the meaning of gay experience. This will entail a willingness to share their views, life histories, and responses. It also involves work. Both require courage and dedication to the cause of enlightening the darkness too many people, straight *and* gay, are constrained to wander in.

Prophecy is a primarily active ministry, however, both in civil society and in the church. Any spirituality which does not eventuate in some form of social action is not authentically Christian. The prophet is called (and often cannot refuse) to criticize, to sensitize, and to protest. The prophet is one who "professes" — who speaks up and speaks out, who will not remain silent in the face of injustice. The prophet is also a transformer, converting awareness and words into action.

In the gay community, active prophecy involves the responsible and productive education of the straight world by an energetic attack on myths, stereotypes, oppressive laws, attitudes, and acts of discrimination. By "responsible," I mean in response to the authentic vocation to prophecy — an ability to listen to the voice of God and to discern the signs of the times. I also mean responsiveness to the actual needs of situations in which fallible human beings find themselves.

The riots that followed the shooting of Harvey Milk and the mild sentencing of Dan White remind us all that gay activists cannot afford the diversion offered by lashing back merely in anger or in the hopeless attempt to achieve full liberation overnight, much less to overcome all opposition and misunderstanding. *Productive* prophecy means, accordingly, efforts having realistic goals which in turn effect real changes; it also means the refusal to be misled by merely symbolic victories and rhetorical consolations.

Prophetic effectiveness likewise entails honesty and good faith — virtues whose absence or weakness among the oppressive majority provides even less excuse for overlooking the real problems of the gay world. Gays and lesbians must address themselves prophetically to the correction of abusive situations in the ghetto, the visible reinforcers of straight fears, myths, and hostility. Social acceptance will remain an ever-retreating hope so long as efforts to reform the position of straight society are vitiated by serious moral deficiencies in the ghetto.

Gay social activists must be accountable, furthermore, to the gay community as a whole. Here the responsibility for assuring accurate representation falls to ordinary men and women who are not militant, but whose destiny is no less involved in the struggle for acceptance than that of their leaders. Similarly, it is vital that the unoutspoken give encouragement and support to their spokesmen and women, whose experiences in city halls and chanceries are often soul-battering. Jesus said, "Anyone who welcomes a prophet because he is a prophet will receive a prophet's reward" (Mt. 10:41).

Mystics and Artists

Listening for the voice of the storm-God of justice and the whispers of the loving Father's compassion ties the acute sensitivity of the artist to the aggressive out-speech of the prophet. Every true prophet is first a mystic, literally "one who closes his eyes" (and mouth) in order to hear and feel the presence of the Friend. And every mystic is an artist — a person of heightened awareness, disciplined in the ways of expressing truth and beauty.

All human beings are probably mystics and artists in the beginning. Most of us simply have it drilled out of us by age five or so by the hum-drum of the "everyday." Gay people are hum-drummed, too, but their constant burden of felt difference, their being rejected in the mind and often at the hands of society prevents them as a group from foreclosing the aesthetic and mystical realms of personality so effectively, simply because they can never fully identify with the greater society. The hum-drummer misses a beat every so often, and in the still moment, when the "beat of a different drummer" can be heard, there is a chance for infinite adventure as the worlds fly apart. Here beauty arises in guises invisible to most. And here, often in the beauty, sometimes in the pain, whispers and thunders the voice of the Lord.

It is no less a surrender to mystification to maintain that gay men and women are more open to God than others — yet, as Jung also recognized, there is a peculiar religious sensitivity among many gays that is distinctive and not too easily dismissed as a substitute for parental love missed in childhood. (The Church has not been a kind mother.) Nonetheless, as with the arts, it is likely though perhaps unprovable, as I have already noted, that a disproportionate number of ministers, priests, sisters, brothers, rabbis, sheiks, and shamans are homosexual — disproportionate so far as the percentage is slightly higher in religion than in other professions.

But mystical sensitivity is not the same as a vocation to the ministry and need not be stifled merely because the Church so often slams the seminary door in gay faces (to its own great loss, I should add). And here arises the need for a gay spirituality that is not identified with a professional "vocation," yet does not exclude it.

JUSTICE AND LOVE

Because Christian spirituality has a twofold foundation in justice and love, the prophetic ministry of justice is not antagonistic to the mystical vocation to love. They complement each other — in fact, require one another. Love, in the Christian ethic, has a kind of primacy, however, and hence it is, I think, that the true prophet is first a mystic, which is to say that real love leads to active "justicing." The love of God which is the beginning, center, and culmination of the mystical life is not separate from human love, which is its emblem and often its medium.

Perceiving God's love in our human loves *is* the Christian mystical experience, just as it is constituted in general by a consciousness of God's presence in moments of ordinary experience: anyone can grovel before a burning bush. Revelation is not a parting of the clouds and a majestic voice, but the sense of presence, the communication of a Self in love and support, an invitation to growth and service.

There are three elements to note with regard to the mystical dimension of life, whether gay or straight: the grace of the present, living for the Kingdom, and the universalization of love. In each case, the structure and the discipline of mystical experience is provided by the exigencies of love. For gays, the ways of creating and sustaining responsible love will be, I think, the essential and ultimate achievement of their spiritual lives. For Christian living means loving rightly — integrating sexuality into the whole of life, subduing love's enemies, and surviving the tests of love. That is to say, loving responsibly, rightfully, and trustingly, despite the unnerving onslaughts of anxiety, jealousy, possessiveness, self-centeredness, and romanticism; enduring the tremendous challenges of unreturned love, loneliness, and the greatest of all human trials, the loss of love. Such *is* the crucible of the spirit, the vessel of God's presence in this life.

Traditionally, the mystical life has been characterized by an acute sensitivity to that presence — not in the past experiences of men and women centuries dead, but in the here and now. Discernment of the grace of the present moment is what distinguishes mystics from those who follow more authoritarian routes, which, whether in literal obedience to scripture or the regimen of liturgy, are both safer and more orthodox. For the outcast and oppressed, however, it is more urgent to grasp what God is doing now and will do in the future than what God has done before.

The future, eschatological element of mystical life is especially relevant for gays and lesbians, whose awareness that they have no lasting city here is perhaps more naturally acute than that of straight persons. Gays may be forever tempted to transform the immediacy and transiency of gay life into a permanent sense of being "out of place." But living for a cause which transcends the physical and temporal limits of the world, whether expressed in specifically religious ways or in the quest for lasting meaning and value — for truth, justice, and well-being — avoids the traps of materialism, sensualism, and surface-existence, and also achieves a continuity surpassing the "ordinary immortality" of procreation and providence.

The eschatological dimension of spiritual life must (and generally is) related to the service of real persons. The great mystics typically translate their love into concrete acts of human devotion, often seeking out the most unfortunate and unwanted members of society. In compassion for their own brothers and sisters, as well as other dispossessed people, a compassion heightened by the struggle against rejection and oppression, gays become able to continue the real tradition of mystical work in the world: prophetic action.

SEND IN THE CLOWNS

It is not mere whimsy that now brings me back to the image of the clown, for in it we find, I think, the embodiment of the artistic, prophetic, and mystical components of gay experience, touched throughout by an uncanny sense of the truly comic character of human life. Whether in modern versions such as those of Lily Tomlin, Jackie Gleason, or Marcel Marceau, or the ancient figure of Mattachine, the Moorish street-fool with his drum, his dance, and his rags, the clown has always signified the will to create through suffering.

Clowns really do not belong in circuses. Like giraffes and elephants, they have been domesticated and rendered innocuous by imprisoning them for entertainment's sake. As our Roman and medieval ancestors knew, clowns belong in the halls of government, on city streets, and in church councils. For they expose human pretensions to divinity and remind the powerful as well as the meek wherein resides our true godliness. But our Calvinistic, Jansenistic moralism with its somber and tragic view of life has banished the jester and the court fool.

Only the saints seem to have preserved the great work of the clown — the Fools in Christ who, in the Eastern church, perform extravagances that demolish the sober pieties of the righteous and undo the real vanities of the all-demanding world. It was the *hilaritas* of their desert forebears which, in the medieval West, left a now-lost heritage of Feasts of Fools and Asses, ceremonies which began on the Feast of the Holy Innocents in December and ended only with Mardi Gras. Recall, too, St.

Philip Neri, a prophet and reformer balancing pillows on his head while dancing for children in the streets of Rome. In our own century, Caryll Houselander, an English mystic and poet with an uncanny ability to calm unmanageable mental patients and prisoners, daubed her face white and prowled the streets of London in quest of Christ's presence in the poor and suffering.

When I see gays as clown figures, I am not attempting to create another stereotype, but to grasp the meaning of a clue as to the deeper significance and worth of homosexuality in civil life and the church.   Here, "clown" is no term of contempt, pity, or amusement — but a title of tremendous importance, of earth-rocking, heaven-shaking seriousness. For despite persecution, suffering, even tragedy, gay men and women continue to endure, to hope, to rise again, and to make festival — showing everyone that life has a meaning if, like Don Quixote, we are foolish enough to believe in it. But if gays are clown-figures, clowns are no less Christ-figures. And the Christian meaning of being gay is to that degree made accessible in grasping the point of clowning.

Clowns liberate us from the tedium of the world's grind; they break down the walls of consciousness, which (we thus discover) are mere paper painted to look like bricks. They hold mirrors before us, not of glass but of action, parodying our even more preposterous poses and posturings, our efforts to seem grave and forbidding as we intimidate our nervous way though life. They raise our levels of insight by displacing our dull and customary viewpoint, so that the incongruity and comedy of life are revealed to us with all the splendid fireworks of Sinai. And here again, in the still, small voice heard in the brief pauses between gasps and applause, we may detect the sound of divine laughter — even in the faint accents of a duck named Donald or an insufficiently suppressed giggle somewhere behind us.

In clowns, we, too, "shoot adown titanic glooms of chasméd fears" — to land in a ludicrous heap. But we rise again, shaken but undaunted and start all over again. And we recognize in clowns the divine clown who, his face caked with the white clay of mourning, his painted tears expressing infinite compassion, yet smiling hugely under the vast grin, will forever rise victorious.

And thus the clowns, the gay clowns of the sexual world who bring all men and women again and again to the revelation, the *re-valuation* of the meaning of sexuality and friendship, of hope and the persistent righting of wrongs, find something of their destiny in celebrating and thus overcoming their misfittingness, their outcastness. And in this, because they are not fundamentally alien, they bring humanity back — and ahead — to itself.

A Clash of Symbols

Given the wide variation in personalities and life styles of gays and lesbians, just as in the straight world, neither a single image, such as that of the clown, nor a single spiritual path can encompass all the areas of personal growth and healing that are involved. Various spiritualities are called for, each of them corresponding to the special needs of different persons in various situations, each no doubt finding expression in a characteristic image or symbol.

For gay Christians, a particularly rich image is found in the Exodus — the pilgrimage of a once-enslaved people freed from the claims of a hostile society but uprooted and on the march toward an uncertain future. The spiritual strengths of Exodus People are hope, confidence, and courage — the readiness to set out on a new and dangerous trek in response to the call of the Spirit.

If the liberation theme of the Exodus is appealing to gay Christians in a special way, as it has been to generations of pilgrims before, so too is the theme of the Eschatological Kingdom, the City of God. Gays are truly a people without an abiding city, for they generally leave no descendants, and family traditions frequently die with them. But, as Jesus told us, such a state is a symbol of those who dedicate themselves wholly to the coming Kingdom, whose bequests are largely spiritual rather than material (cf. Mt. 19:10-12). Gays, for this reason, are tremendously *free* — they have a large measure of independence and liberty which can be used to build the Lasting City, or can be wasted and abused, squandered on short-term enjoyment.

The Bible abounds with such dynamic symbols, and their spiritual significance is much richer than any kind of technical depiction. Even the apparently mundane clowns raise our consciousness symbolically by reflecting social patterns — especially roles and stereotypes we are ordinarily unable, because we are unwilling, to see. They don't need to do it deliberately; their gift is simply to do it so well that they make us uncomfortable — more so to the degree that we are unwittingly *controlled* by social images, roles, and stereotypes such as the Macho Male, the Seductive Mistress, or the Helpless Naïf. Clowns reveal the games people play by exaggerating them to the point of visibility.

Revealing the demonic dimension of dominant social forces is a truly prophetic function. The great Jewish prophets often parodied the Jews' attitudes and predicted the outcome of their conduct symbolically — much as the classic clowns have done. Examples are not hard to find, such as Isaiah's naming his children symbolically; Jeremiah's celibacy and behavioral parodies — burying his loincloth and breaking the clay pots; Ezekiel's becoming mute, his gestures with the frying pan and shaving his beard and hair, and his parable of the dry bones; or Hosea's marrying and reclaiming a prostitute.

Through this symbolic process, the prophets personally and publicly identified themselves with the whole people of Israel. But their teaching far outlived the historical circumstances in which they lived and taught, not only because people haven't changed their basic attitudes all that much, but also because the universal dimension of the prophets' teaching was captured and expressed in the ordinary symbols they used.

The specifying religious symbol that perhaps best expresses the meaning of being gay within the Christian community today is neither the Clown nor the Prophet, however, although both functions remain alive and effective in gay Christian experience.

Rather, I have come to see it in the biblical figure which became the favorite image of the early Church in describing the meaning of Jesus' suffering and death — Isaiah's figure of the Servant of Yahweh — the Suffering Servant.

ON SERVICE AND SUFFERING

In the chapter 53 of the Book of Isaiah we find the fourth song of the servant of Yahweh. It was apparently first intended to represent the redeeming suffering of Israel itself, possibly even that of the prophet, but in the eyes of the early Christians, the image found perfect fulfillment in the life of Jesus. It still finds fulfillment in the lives of all those whose suffering at the hands of the so-called righteous bring men and women to a new understanding of love and justice and the real wideness in God's mercy. This is especially true in view of the AIDS crisis:

He was despised and rejected by men;
  a man of sorrows, and acquainted with grief;
as one from whom men hide their faces
  he was despised, and we esteemed him not.

Surely he has borne our griefs and carried our sorrows;
  Yet we esteemed him stricken, smitten by God, and afflicted.
But he was wounded for our transgressions,
  he was bruised for our iniquities;
upon him was the chastisement that made us whole,
  and with his stripes we are healed.
All we like sheep have gone astray;
  we have turned every one to his own way;
and the Lord has laid on him the iniquity of us all.

He was oppressed and he was afflicted,
  yet he opened not his mouth;
like a lamb that is led to the slaughter,
  and like a sheep that before its shearers is dumb,
  so he opened not his mouth.
By oppression and judgment he was taken away;

and as for his generation, who considered
that he was cut off out of the land of the living,
stricken for the transgression of my people?
And they made his grave with the wicked
and with a rich man in his death,
although he had done no violence,
And there was no deceit in his mouth (vv. 3-9).

It isn't necessary here to illustrate in great detail the actual and often continual suffering that is imposed on gays simply because they are gay — they are called sick, immoral, and criminals, they are rejected by family and associates, disgraced and despised by the law, frequently denied due process and equal protection. They are deprived of housing, fired from their jobs, refused employment, and harassed when they do find work. Such persecution is amplified in the case of those also suffering from AIDS. All too often, religious figures add publicly to the weight of rejection by denunciations and condemnations, much like those of Anita Bryant's sad crusade a few years ago and those being repeated today by evangelists like Rev. Jerry Falwell.

Gays are generally held by such people to be "smitten and afflicted" by God, especially when they have contracted AIDS. And, also like the servant of the Lord, most gays simply have to suffer in silence, for there is no one to turn to. Condemned by society, family, and religion, they can find minimal acceptance only in the companionship of other gays and sometimes that of similar outcasts, such as artists and street-people, who are also rejected by society simply because they are different. Outwardly similar to everyone else and consequently presumed to be straight, gay men and women must often bear silently the scorn and ridicule of jokes and malicious gossip. Their crucifixion is an inner one for the most part, but often transformed into overt persecution as well if they admit their orientation or merely become suspect, much less identify themselves as a person with AIDS.

The reason I think the song of the servant of Yahweh applies in particular to lesbians and gay men is because of the crucial middle verses: "he was wounded for our transgressions and bruised for our iniquities." Here is why gays are so widely scorned and persecuted in our society. For *by their very existence* they prophetically raise to consciousness the inordinately sinful and truly demonic preoccupation with genital sexuality that so characterizes our culture as a whole. They do this by being sexually different, by *not* sharing in the Ken-and-Barbie-doll charade that dominates the entertainment industries and mass media.

The claim that homosexuality is not only a deviation, but a *threat* which must be eradicated, testifies to the underlying insecurity permeating the whole sexual merry-go-round. I remain convinced that the real problem of homosexuality is, in fact, the frustration of a society desperately unsure of itself sexually and thus ready to lash out at any suspected deviation — including celibacy. The gay man or woman is thus doubly the victim of a society uneasy about sex. Lesbians and gays come to embody this uneasiness symbolically and therefore become the target for the anger and fear spread throughout the straight world, forces not diminished by the specter of AIDS.

By accepting their homosexuality as the price of their solidarity with the human family as a whole, gays — whether they know it or not — also take upon themselves the full weight of the sexual tension of man and womankind. By learning to live with their gayness, they can help others learn to be more accepting of their own sexuality as it is — not as the image-makers project it in their video and celluloid fantasy worlds. Gay women and men can thus absorb and release the powerful, sometimes violent energy of the emotional conflicts created by the collision of artificial images of human sexuality and the real situation men and women find themselves in. And so, gays can also bring *healing* into the vast sexual dis-ease that tortures contemporary society despite its pretensions of liberation. Thus, the song of the Servant of Yahweh continues, "Upon him was the chastisement that made us whole, and with his stripes we are healed."

Lesbians and gay men may never see their situation in this

light, of course.   They may even come to hate themselves, reject their sexuality, and grow to hate society and their own families, perhaps even God.   They can give in to the sexual stereotypes of the straight world and merely translate them into gay terms. But neither the witness nor the suffering will go away because of self-rejection.   Nor will they go away because it is also possible to go to the other extreme and revel in promiscuity and every thinkable form of sexual outlet. Ultimately, suffering can acquire meaning only because it is *creative*, and as such, can be taken up in a broader and richer experience of life.

Suffering is not intrinsically creative. It can only be *made* creative — and therefore redemptive — by being willingly accepted as a sign of compassion and solidarity. And only a profound *love* can make suffering creative and redemptive. This is the mystery revealed in the life and death of Jesus of Nazareth and made effective for us all in his resurrection as the Christ.

The meaning of homosexual experience, then, is the creativity of suffering made possible by deep love — and by that love, overcoming suffering, not avoiding it. Suffering must be gone *through* — not around. Resurrection means that on the other side of suffering willingly undergone as a sign of our solidarity with all men and women is the reality of a greater joy and peace. These are not to be postponed until some future time: they are possible *now* — the joy of being gay found in self-acceptance, in awareness of being one *with* other men and women and, in a true sense their representative, and the peace made in loving creatively and effectively. The great power of the gay person and the gay community lies in the potential to love — to love beyond the surface tension of immediate gratification, and to love despite suffering and rejection at the hands of the persons whose lives are immeasurably enriched by the fact there *are* gay persons around to love them and to suffer for them.

Far from being the curse of an angry god, the AIDS epidemic has become an occasion for compassion, outreach, and hope. The face of God revealed by AIDS is not that of the

Grand Inquisitor, but of the Suffering Servant. AIDS is another cross, whose open arms have drawn Infinite Love back into the world not to condemn or to destroy, but to heal. And in order to heal, Infinite Love has again found place by being lifted up onto that gibbet itself. From there alone could Divine Pity draw all human beings upward. "For mercy has a human heart,/ Pity a human face;/ and love the human form divine;/ And peace the human dress."[4] To see the human face of God today, we need only minister to someone with AIDS.

Thus, the joy of being gay is found not only in the comic vision of humanity so essential to Christianity and symbolized in the figure of the clown desperately and bravely struggling to overcome the oppressive forces of society by mocking them. It is also found in the tragic vision of the faithful but suffering servant who patiently endures even death, knowing that his or her agony takes away something of the sin of the world, and that vindication will come in God's way, and in God's time. But the comic vision, even though it is corrected by the tragic vision, is more fundamental, for like Christian faith itself, it rests on the premise and the *experience* that love is stronger than hate, life stronger than death, joy stronger than sadness. The comic vision believes that restitution *will* come. It is the very foundation of hope.

Tragedy corrects comedy by endowing it with the tension of expectation, the suspense of anticipated victory in the midst of evident defeat, the ground for hope and struggle. That is not to say that tragedy is less real than comedy — any gay woman or man can tell you otherwise (as can anyone else who has lived beyond the edge of superficiality). It *is* to claim that every tragedy — AIDS included — is only temporary and provisional, and that ultimate resolution in joy, love, and fulfillment, the unifying *comus* at the end of the play, is the final episode of what is in truth a divine comedy.

NOTES

1. See, for example, John Harvey, *The Homosexual Person*, op. cit., pp. 103, 113.
2. See Bell and Weinberg, *Homosexualities*, pp. 199, 208-09, 215, and Karlen, op. cit., pp. 526-33.
3. See, for instance, Michael Shnayerson, "One by One," *Vanity Fair*, March 1987, pp. 91-154.
4. William Blake, *Songs of Innocence*, XX: "The Divine Image."

POSTLUDE

Resources for Further Study

1. BOOKS AND MEDIA

Gloria Guss Back, *Are You Still My Mother? Are You Still My Family?* New York: Warner Books, 1987.

Derrick Sherwin Bailey, *Homosexuality and the Western Christian Tradition*, Hamden, CT: Archon Press, 1975.

Edward Batchelor, Jr., ed., *Homosexuality and Ethics*, New York: Pilgrim Press, 1980.

Alan P. Bell and Martin S. Weinberg, *Homosexualities: A Study of Diversity among Men and Women*, New York: Simon and Schuster, 1978.

John Boswell, *Christianity, Social Tolerance, and Homosexuality*, Chicago: University of Chicago Press, 1980.

B. R. Burg, *Sodomy and the Pirate Tradition: English Sea Rovers in the Seventeenth-Century Caribbean*, New York and London: New York University Press, 1984.

Don Clark, *Living Gay*, Millbrae, CA: Celestial Arts, 1979.

——, *The New Loving Someone Gay*, Millbrae, CA: Celestial Arts, revised ed., 1987.

Wainwright Churchill, *Homosexual Behavior among Males*, Englewood Cliffs, NJ: Prentice-Hall, 1971.

Vicky Cosstick, ed., *AIDS: Meeting the Community Challenge*, Middlegreen, Slough: St. Paul Publications, 1987.

Rosemary Curb and Nancy Manahan, eds., *Lesbian Nuns: Breaking the Silence*, Tallahassee: Naiad Press, 1985.

Declaration on Certain Questions concerning Sexual Ethics (*Persona Humana*), Sacred Congregation for the Doctrine of the Faith, Dec. 29, 1975.

Jack Dominian, *The Church and the Sexual Revolution*, London: Darton, Longman, and Todd, 1973.

——, *Proposals for a New Sexual Ethic*, London: Darton, Longman, and Todd, 1977.

George R. Edwards, *Gay/Lesbian Liberation: A Biblical Perspective*, New York: Pilgrim Press, 1984.

Ronald M. Enroth and Gerald E. Jamison, *The Gay Church*, Grand Rapids: Wm. B. Eerdmans, 1974.

Frances Fitzgerald, *Cities on a Hill*, New York: Simon and Schuster, 1986.

John Fortunato, *AIDS: The Spiritual Dilemma*, San Francisco: Harper and Row, 1987.

——, *Embracing the Exile*, New York: Seabury, 1982.

Michael Goodich, *The Unmentionable Vice: Homosexuality in the Later Medieval Period*, Santa Barbara and Oxford: Clio Press, 1979.

Betty Fairchild and Nancy Hayward, *Now that You Know: What Every Parent Should Know about Homosexuality*, New York: Harcourt Brace Jovanovich, 1979.

Eileen P. Flynn, *AIDS: A Catholic Call for Compassion*, Kansas City: Sheed and Ward, 1985.

John Gallagher, ed., *Homosexuality and the Magisterium: Documents from the Vatican and the U.S. Bishops 1975-1985*, Mt. Rainier, MD: New Ways Ministry, 1986.

Donald Goergen, O.P., *The Sexual Celibate*, New York: The Seabury Press, 1974.

Jeannine Gramick, ed., *Homosexuality and the Catholic Church*, Mt. Rainier, MD: New Ways Ministry, 1983.

Carolyn Welch Griffin, Marian J. Wirth, Arthur G. Wirth, *Beyond Acceptance: Parents of Lesbians and Gays Talk about Their Experiences*, Englewood Cliffs, NJ: Prentice-Hall, 1986.

Joe Halloran, *Understanding Homosexual Persons: Straight Answers from Gays*, Hickesville, NY: Exposition Press, 1979.

Martin Hoffman *The Gay World: The Social Creation of Evil*, New York: Bantam, 1969.

An Introduction to the Pastoral Care of Homosexual People, Catholic Social Welfare Commission, Catholic Bishops of England and Wales (1980), Mt. Rainier, Md: New Ways Ministry, 1981.

Arno Karlen, *Sexuality and Homosexuality: A New View*, New York: W.W. Norton, 1971.

Jerry Kirk, *The Homosexual Crisis in the Mainline Church: A Presbyterian Minister Speaks Out*, Nashville: Thomas Nelson, 1978.

Letter to the Bishops of the Catholic Church on the Pastoral Care of Homosexual Persons, Sacred Congregation for the Doctrine of the Faith, October 1, 1986, Washington: United States Catholic Conference, 1986.

Richard Lovelace, *Homosexuality and the Church: Crisis, Conflict, Compassion,* Old Tappan, NJ: Revell, 1978.

John Macmurray, *Reason and Emotion,* London: Faber and Faber, 1967.

Malcolm Macourt, ed., *Towards a Theology of Gay Liberation,* London: SCM Press, Ltd., 1977.

Judd Marmor, ed., *Homosexual Behavior: A Modern Reappraisal,* New York: Basic Books, Inc., 1980.

William H. Masters and Virginia E. Johnson, *Homosexuality in Perspective,* Boston: Little, Brown and Co., 1979.

Brian McNaught, *A Disturbed Peace: Selected Writings of an Irish Catholic Homosexual,* Washington: Dignity, Inc., 1981.

John McNeill, *The Church and the Homosexual,* Kansas City: Sheed, McMeel and Andrews, 1976.

Elizabeth Moberly, *Homosexuality: A New Christian Ethic* Greenwood, SC: Attic Press, 1983.

————, *Psychogenesis: The Early Development of Gender Identity,* London: Routledge and Kegan Paul, 1983.

Betty Clare Moffatt et al., eds., *AIDS: A Self-Care Manual,* Santa Monica, CA: IBS Press, 1987.

Ann Muller, *Parents Matter: Parents' Relationships with Lesbian Daughters and Gay Sons,* Tallahassee: Naiad Press, 1987.

James B. Nelson, *Embodiment*, Minneapolis: Augsburg Publishing Co., 1978, especially "Gayness and Homosexuality: Issues for the Church," also reprinted in Batchelor, ed. cit., pp. 186-210.

Robert Nugent, SDS, ed., *A Challenge to Love*, New York: Crossroad, 1986.

W. D. Oberholtzer, ed., *Is Gay Good?* Philadelphia: The Westminster Press, 1972.

Tom O'Connor, with Ahmed Gonzalez-Nunez, *Living with AIDS: Reaching Out*, San Francisco: Corwin Publishers, 1987.

Troy Perry with Charles L. Lucas, *The Lord Is My Shepherd and He Knows I'm Gay*, New York: Bantam, 1973.

W. Norman Pittenger, *Making Sexuality Human*, Philadelphia: Pilgrim Press, 1970.

———, *Time for Consent*, London: SCM Press, 1970.

———, *Gay Lifestyles: A Christian Interpretation of Homosexuality and the Homosexual*, Los Angeles: The Universal Fellowship Press, 1977.

Benjamin Sadock et. al., eds., *The Sexual Experience*, Baltimore: Williams and Wilkins Co., 1976.

Letha Scanzoni and Virginia Ramey Mollencott, *Is the Homosexual My Neighbor?* New York: Harper and Row, 1980.

Robin Scroggs, *The New Testament and Homosexuality: Contextual Background for Contemporary Debate*, Philadelphia: Fortress Press, 1983.

Charles Silverstein, *A Family Matter: A Parent's Guide to Homosexuality*, New York: McGraw-Hill, 1977.

June Singer, *Androgyny: Toward a New Theory of Sexuality*, Garden City, NY: Doubleday Anchor Books, 1977.

Mark Thompson, ed., *Gay Spirit: Myth and Meaning*, New York: St. Martin's Press, 1987.

Joan Timmerman, *The Mardi Gras Syndrome: Rethinking Christian Sexuality*, New York: Crossroad, 1984.

Keith Vacha, *Quiet Fire: Memoirs of Older Gay Men*, ed. by Cassie Damewood, Trumansburg, NY: Crossing Press, 1985.

C. V. Tripp, *The Homosexual Matrix*, New York: Signet, 1977.

Ginny Vida, ed., *Our Right to Love: A Lesbian Resource Book*, Englewood Cliffs, NJ: Prentice-Hall, 1978.

George Weinberg, *Society and the Healthy Homosexual*, Garden City, NY: Doubleday Anchor Books, 1973.

Martin S. Weinberg and Colin J. Williams, *Male Homosexuals: Their Problems and Adaptations*, New York: Oxford University Press, 1974.

Ralph W. Weltge, ed., *The Same Sex*, Philadelphia: Pilgrim Press, 1969.

James D. Whitehead and Evelyn Eaton Whitehead, *Christian Life Patterns*, Garden City, New York: Doubleday and Co., 1982.

James D. Whitehead and Evelyn Eaton Whitehead, "The Shape of Compassion: Reflections on Catholics and Homosexuality," *Spirituality Today* 39, 2 (Summer, 1987): 126-36.

Bruce Williams, O.P., "Homosexuality: The New Vatican Statement," *Theological Studies* 48, 2 (June, 1987): 259-77.

Barbara Zanotti, ed., *A Faith of Our Own: Explorations by Catholic Lesbians*, Trumansburg, NY: The Crossing Press, 1986.

Fiction:

Rita Mae Brown, *Rubyfruit Jungle*, New York: Bantam, 1977.

Aidan Chambers, *Dance on My Grave*, New York: Harper and Row, 1986.

Andrew Halloran, *Dancer from the Dance*, New York: New American Library, 1982.

Wallace Hamilton, *Coming Out*, New York: Signet, 1977.

Armistead Maupin, *Tales of the City*, New York: Harper & Row, 1982.

————, *More Tales of the City,*, New York: Harper & Row, 1982.

————, *Further Tales of the City*, New York: Harper & Row, 1983.

————, *Babycakes*, New York: Harper & Row, 1985.

————, *Significant Others*, New York: Harper & Row, 1987.

John Reid, *The Best Little Boy in the World*, New York: Ballantine, 1976.

Vincent Virga, *A Comfortable Corner*, New York: Avon, 1986.

Alice Walker, *The Color Purple*, New York: Washington Square Press, 1983.

Patricia Nell Warren, *The Beauty Queen*, New York: William Morrow, 1978.

Drama:

The AIDS Show
As Is
Bent
The Fifth of July
March of the Falsettos
The Normal Heart
Streamers
Torch Song Trilogy

Video:

On Being Gay: A Conversation with Brian McNaught, TRB Productions, P.O. Box 2362, Boston, MA   02107 (VHS or Beta format), $39.95 plus $3.00 postage and handling.

Films:

The Boys in the Band
The Children's Hour
Consenting Adult (made for television)
The Killing of Sister George
The L-Shaped Room
Making Love
Maurice
My Beautiful Laundrette
The Naked Civil Servant
Personal Best
Sunday Bloody Sunday
A Taste of Honey
The Times of Harvey Milk
The Truth about Alex (made for television)
Waiting for the Moon
Word is Out

2. NATIONAL ORGANIZATIONS

A. Religious organizations:

Affirmation (Gay and Lesbian Mormons)
Box 26302
San Francisco, CA   94126
(415) 641-4554

Affirmation (United Methodists for Gay and Lesbian
   Concerns)
Box 1021
Evanston, IL   60204
(312) 475-0499

American Baptists Concerned
870 Erie St.
Oakland, CA   94610
(415) 564-8652

Brethren/Mennonite Council for Gay Concerns
Box 65724
Washington, DC   20035
(202) 462-2595

Catholic Coalition for Gay Civil Rights
Box 1985
New York, NY   10159
(201) 845-5907

Conference for Catholic Lesbians
Box 436, Planetarium Station
New York, NY   10024
(212) 595-2768

Courage
c/o Rev. John Harvey, OSFS
St. Michael's Rectory
424 W. 34th St.
New York, NY 10001
(212) 421-0426

Dignity, Inc.
1500 Massachusetts Ave. NW
Suite 11
Washington, DC 20005
(202) 861-0017

Evangelical Outreach Ministries
Box 7882
Atlanta, GA 30357
(404) 288-5801

Evangelicals Concerned
c/o Dr. Ralph Blair
30 E. 60th St.
Suite 1403
New York, NY 10022
(212) 688-0628

Friends for Lesbian and Gay Concerns (Quakers)
Box 222
Sunneytown, PA 18084
(215) 234-8424

International Conference of Gay and Lesbian Jews
Box 881272
San Francisco, CA 94188

Lutherans Concerned/ North America
Box 10461
Chicago, IL 60610

New Ways Ministry
4012 29th St.
Mt. Rainier, MD   20822
(301) 277-5674

Presbyterians for Gay/Lesbian Concerns
c/o James D. Anderson
Box 38
New Brunswick, NJ   08903
(201) 846-1510

Seventh Day Adventist Kinship International, Inc.
Box 3840
Los Angeles, CA   90078
(213) 876-2076

Sovereignty (Jehovah's Witnesses)
Box 27242
Santa Ana, CA   92799

Unitarian Universalists for Lesbian/Gay Concerns
Box 1077
Back Bay Station
Boston, MA   02108
(617) 742-2100

United Church Coalition for Lesbian/Gay Concerns
18 N. College St.
Athens, Ohio   45701
(614) 593-7301

United Lesbian and Gay Christian Scientists
Box 2171
Beverly Hills, CA   90212
(213) 465-6079

Universal Fellowship of Metropolitan Community Churches (MCC)
5300 Santa Monica Blvd., #304
Los Angeles, CA 90029
(213) 464-5100

B. Service organizations

AIDS Action Council
Box 1396
Washington, DC 20077
(202) 628-4160

FUND For Human Dignity
666 Broadway, 4th flr.
New York, NY 10012
(212) 529-1600.

Gay and Lesbian Alcoholism Services, Inc.
Box 1141
Cooper Stn.
New York, NY 10276

Gay Task Force
American Library Association
Box 2383
Philadelphia, PA 19103

Federation of Parents and Friends of Lesbians and Gays, Inc.
Box 24565
Los Angeles, CA 90024
(213) 472-8952

National AIDS Hotline:
(800) 342-AIDS (24 hours)

National Gay/Lesbian Crisisline:
(800) 221-7044 (Mon-Fri 3-9 PM)

National Association of Lesbian & Gay Alcoholism
  Professionals
204 W. 20th St.
New York, NY 10011

National Federation of Parents and Friends of Gays
8020 Eastern Ave. NW
Washington, DC 20012
(202) 726-3223

National Gay and Lesbian Task Force
1517 U St. N.W.
Washington, DC 20009
(202) 332-6483

Index